Olcott

MORE PRAISE FOR *GETTING SMART*

"Some people believe private industry has no place in education. *Getting Smart* makes a persuasive case that private investment and innovation can *and will* transform schools for the better and provides a compelling map for both educators and investors."

—John Katzman, chief executive officer, 2tor, Inc.

"Rocketship pioneered the hybrid school model, using a combination of traditional classroom and individualized learning to eliminate the achievement gap in a more efficient, sustainable, and scalable manner. Tom's book does a great job of explaining how the next generation of charter networks like ours will provide the solutions to eliminate the achievement gap in our lifetimes."

—John Danner, CEO, Rocketship Education

"We better get smart about *Getting Smart*. This is just-in-time learning that practitioners and policymakers need to implement. The sooner the better."

—Elliot Washor, EdD, codirector, Big Picture Learning

"This is a refreshing overview of one of the biggest problems facing us in the United States and of the strategies that can catapult us past it to educate the talent critical to our future. In the twenty-five years I've worked with countless education market firms and leaders, few can match the vision, intelligence, entrepreneurial skill, political savvy, reach, and commitment to making positive changes to education of Tom Vander Ark. He uses it all and more to write this prescription for moving ahead. It's not rocket science or pie in the sky. It's about unleashing the creative talent and constructive energy in our kids, teachers, administrators, parents, and government with skills for the twenty-first century and beyond. U.S. economic competitiveness? It ain't hardly over yet. You won't be sorry you've read it."

—Nelson B. Heller, PhD, president, EdNET/Heller Report

"Tom Vander Ark's amazing description of the 'digital revolution' coming at American K–12 should get states acting to maximize its potential—perhaps generating autonomous schools free to innovate with the new technology. 'Digital' can personalize, helping improve both learning and the system's economics. Legislators take note."

—Ted Kolderie and Joe Graba, Education|Evolving

"*Getting Smart* shines a light on challenges facing the U.S. education system but doesn't stall out there. Rather, it homes in on solutions and opportunities in front of us through digital learning. Tom Vander Ark is one of the brightest, most passionate, and visionary education advocates in our midst with the gift of being able to organize key message points and paint a picture of exciting and engaging personalized learning experiences that will transform teaching and learning. Consider the shifts and drivers moving us toward transformation. Reflect on Tom's predictions one, five, and ten years out. Educators, policy makers, and parents are considering digital and blended learning. Our young people are already there—it's time the rest of us catch up! As Tom says, 'The revolution is on.'"

—Vicki Smith Bigham, president, Bigham Technology Solutions, Inc.,
and EdNET Conference Manager, MDR

"Tom Vander Ark earns his merit badge showing us where the parts to the new learning ecosystem are. As William Gibson noted, 'The future is already here—it's just unevenly distributed,' and finding those clues to the future is hard work. Fortunately, Tom has done the detective work weaving together the fabric of the digital revolution that is going on already. He shows how today's innovations will link and become the transformative 'killer apps' of the future. He finds the leading edge—and finds much of it is being led by the learners themselves!"

—Myk Garn, director, Educational Technology Cooperative,
Southern Regional Education Board

"*Getting Smart* is a must-read for educational leaders. It explores exactly how today's students are different; how learning has changed; why, where, and how we still need to change; and more. Tom Vander Ark identifies key drivers that are forcing change and provides a detailed analysis of a wide variety of emerging learning programs, systems, and products—all with the view of today's new reality in terms of learning."

—Julie Young, president and CEO, Florida Virtual School

"Anyone over twenty-five, parents, and educators alike will gain insight into the rapidly evolving field of digital learning and the very real world in which our children are growing up. In order to educate our children we need to understand the many opportunities in their world and recognize they are different from their parents."

—Samuel H. Smith, Washington State University

GETTING SMART

HOW DIGITAL LEARNING IS CHANGING THE WORLD

TOM VANDER ARK

Foreword by Governor Bob Wise

JOSSEY-BASS
A Wiley Imprint
www.josseybass.com

Published by Jossey-Bass
A Wiley Imprint
989 Market Street, San Francisco, CA 94103-1741—www.josseybass.com

Jossey-Bass books and products are available through most bookstores. To contact Jossey-Bass directly call our Customer Care Department within the U.S. at 800-956-7739, outside the U.S. at 317-572-3986, or fax 317-572-4002.

Wiley also publishes its books in a variety of electronic formats and by print-on-demand. Some material included with standard print versions of this book may not be included in e-books or in print-on-demand. If the version of this book that you purchased references media such as CD or DVD that was not included in your purchase, you may download this material at http://booksupport.wiley.com. For more information about Wiley products, visit www.wiley.com.

Library of Congress Cataloging-in-Publication Data

Vander Ark, Tom, date.
   Getting smart : how digital learning is changing the world / Tom Vander Ark ; foreword by Bob Wise.—1st ed.
      p. cm.
   Includes bibliographical references and index.
    ISBN 978-1-118-00723-5 (cloth); ISBN 978-1-118-11585-5 (ebk.);
    ISBN 978-1-118-11586-2 (ebk.); ISBN 978-1-118-11587-9 (ebk.)
    1. Computer-assisted instruction—United States.   2. Internet in education—
United States.   3. Blended learning—United States.   I. Title.
LB1028.5.V26   2011
371.33'40973—dc23   2011024028

Printed in the United States of America
FIRST EDITION
HB Printing   10 9 8 7 6 5 4 3 2 1

For students from Newark to Nairobi

CONTENTS

CONTENTS

FOREWORD
Governor Bob Wise

During the past two decades, West Virginia's leaders in government and education worked hard to wire our schools and made sure students had access to technology. Our state became a national leader in educational technology. I'm proud of the work our teachers and principals did. They opened up the world for many students and brought foreign language instruction into the most remote parts of the state. It deepened and expanded learning for many students but it didn't result in a significant difference in traditionally measured outcomes. And it added to the growing cost of educating our students.

The situation is much different today. Learning tools are better and cheaper and there is more clarity around the problems that we're trying to solve. In fact, early in 2010, I came to the conclusion that this country faced three educational challenges that would not be solved by conventional means: global skill demands versus current educational attainment, the funding cliff faced by most states, and a looming teacher shortage.

These are tough problems, but technology can help—specifically learning online. In June 2010, the Alliance for

Excellent Education published the *Online Learning Imperative* with the core premise that "[t]he current process and infrastructure for educating students in this country cannot sustain itself any longer."[1] Since publication, I've been on a national campaign to help schools and policy makers explore new ways to solve some vexing problems. Following is a short discussion of each of the problems and how online learning will be part of the solution.

Despite growing investment, U.S. academic achievement and high school completion rates have been essentially flat for several decades. Specific reform strategies show promise but the system is pretty resistant. Producing and sustaining educational quality at scale has proven to be a vexing challenge; yet online learning is a massively scalable solution to provide standards-based curriculum, effective teaching, and flexible delivery. As Tom points out, personal digital learning holds the promise of customized and engaging learning—we both think these factors can change the learning curve and ignite a decade of significant academic improvement.

The residual of the Great Recession and subsequent stimulus funding was a "funding cliff" that most states experienced beginning in 2011. As Secretary of Education Arne Duncan has suggested, the "new normal" will be an extended period of constrained resources and increasing academic demands. As noted in the *Imperative,* "As technology has revolutionized the way Americans get news, communicate, listen to music, shop, and do business, now is the time for American students in thousands of underperforming classrooms to realize the same gains."[2] The only way we can get better results for less money is to leverage the power of learning online. Schools such as Rocketship and Carpe Diem that blend online and on-site learning are demonstrating that it's possible to structure schools in new and more productive ways.

The last big challenge is the goal of a great teacher in every classroom in America—critically important but not possible, at least not without technology. I frequently point out that there are eighty-eight certified physics teachers in Georgia and 440 high schools. As we push more students into higher-level math and science, we need to use online learning to extend the reach and impact of our nation's best teachers and ensure that every student has access to the best courses and the best instruction.

President Obama has been talking about "winning the future." And at the Alliance, we know that starts with education. Former Florida governor Jeb Bush and I cochair Digital Learning Now!, which in December 2010 issued a report outlining the path forward for state policy makers.

As the Alliance team campaigns for excellence and equity, we have the good fortune to work with the Foundation for Excellence in Education; Susan Patrick, president and CEO of the International Association for K–12 Online Learning; Michael Horn, leader of the Innosight Institute; and Tom Vander Ark's team. We appreciate Michael's contribution in coauthoring *Disrupting Class*[3] and his advocacy for innovation. *Getting Smart* builds on and extends that work and describes the historic pivot to personal digital learning.

Tom and I have been at this for a while and know how hard it is to improve public delivery systems, but we're both optimistic that online learning will drive dramatic progress in this coming decade for American education, with millions of young people getting the quality education so vital for them and our nation.

PREFACE

Why This Book Now?

This book deals with the most important subject in the world—learning. The arc of human history will be bent by learning—specifically, the proportion of the seven billion people on the planet who have the knowledge and skills to support their family, make thoughtful choices, and participate in self-governance. The alternative consequences of mass illiteracy and ignorance in the United States and around the globe are dire. If we can help enough people get smart, I believe we can confront the challenges of climate change, public health, peace, and security.

Learning is the big change lever. I'm glad there are people who have dedicated their lives to fighting poverty and disease, to conservation and security, but in the long run our only hope for a sustainable future is helping more people get smart. That's why I wrote this book and why I spend all of my time working on and writing about innovations that will extend quality learning experiences to those who don't have access to them today.

What's happening around the edges makes me very optimistic. The Internet has changed the opportunity set; as access to broadband expands, devices become cheaper, and learning content gets better, it's almost possible for anyone to learn any-thing.[1] Dramatic advances in informal learning (for example, Google Search, Wikipedia), military and corporate training, and growth of online learning make me very confident that we can improve the quality of education in the United States without a big increase in investment. Perhaps even more important, we are very close to being able to build new tools and schools that will reach the next billion—young people in places that historically have had little or no educational opportunity.

What makes me qualified to tell you about learning? I don't have the traditional qualifications to discuss this topic but I have a point of view informed by some interesting experiences, so allow me to introduce myself.

I'm an engineer by original training and spent a lot of the first few years of my career underground in Colorado and Penn-sylvania coal mines managing construction projects. I still find great satisfaction in imagining how a system can work better and being part of implementing the solution. Engineering school taught me to work hard and to be systematic about problem solving—two things that have served me well.

Drawn by the deep satisfaction of creating the spark of learn-ing for another person, some people know early that they are called to teach. I did not feel the pull until after I finished an MBA and got the sense that there had to be a better way to con-struct a series of learning experiences that prepared young people for careers in business. Frustrated by boring and disconnected classes, on graduation day I walked into the dean's office and said, "That sucked." He asked me to help make it better. I spent a couple evenings a week over the next seven years as an adjunct instructor at two universities in Denver trying to make business education more applied, more engaging, and more integrated.

At twenty-six I thought I was smart enough to launch my own consulting firm. It proved to be a big failure but a great learning experience. In 1987, I joined a retail start-up in a new category called membership warehouse (like Costco and Sam's Club) just as the concept took off. As a senior executive of what quickly became a multibillion-dollar company, I found myself in the CEO's office one day being instructed to adopt a children's charity in Denver and take them to the next level. It seemed like an odd request and an imposition for a self-centered young man with goals. I picked a wonky-sounding research and advocacy group called Colorado Children's Campaign. After ninety days of reading data reports and visiting high-poverty schools with the executive direct, Barbara O'Brien, I had a full-on conversion—she made me a learning evangelist. I had spent almost fifteen years worrying about the next job, the next car, and the next house and suddenly I had a new mission that I was passionate about and a good sense of the kind of work I enjoyed doing. After we sold the company to Kmart, I knew I would spend the rest of my career in education—I just had no idea where or how to start.

In 1994, after seven hundred days of contemplating this new education mission (while helping telecom companies implement new technology), the opportunity knocked. A friend called in July as we were walking out the door on vacation and said, "I'm doing a search for a school district in Washington State. I convinced them to interview a nontraditional candidate and I can't find one. Would you apply?" I laughed and after a short discussion, as a favor, I told him he could submit my name. When we returned six days later, there were six messages on my answering machine. The last said, "You are a finalist, you need to be in Seattle tomorrow." Long story short, three weeks later I moved my family to Federal Way, a city between Seattle and Tacoma. The teachers went on strike my first day as superintendent; they had been at an impasse with the district for some time but I think my presence just made it too good an opportunity for the state association to pass up. I spent the first week meeting teachers on the picket line during the day and holding open-microphone town hall meetings at night—the strike turned out to be a great way get to know the community.

The second big shock (after the strike): no data. I was used to morning sales reports by store by item. This was before state standards and end-of-year assessments. So the first thing we did was to identify twenty-four key performance indicators, half academic and half covering staff and customer satisfaction and financial, operating, and safety measures. By my fourth year as superintendent, we had introduced new options and made progress against every metric we tracked but it was clear that the three-year plan would take a decade to complete. We had not restructured our high schools. Efforts to introduce standards-based report cards resulted in a no-confidence vote. Attempts to push budgets and autonomy to schools had assumed too much about capacity.

The work improving schools is intensely personal for students, families, and teachers; it is unbelievably political and complicated by layers of bureaucracy. Being a public school superintendent is the best and worst job in the world simultaneously—the rewards are great but so is the pain. It is far more complicated than running a billion-dollar corporation. Although the leadership agenda is similar to that of the private sector, the people who work in education are different—they bring a sense of mission and sign up for a different employment bargain. As a result, an incentive strategy that works in business won't be received and work the same way in education.

After my fifth year as superintendent, I had the opportunity to join a small new family foundation, the Gates Library Foundation. A few months into the assignment, it was merged with another family fund to create the Bill & Melinda Gates Foundation. I told the cochairs that I thought it would take $2 billion to make a difference. Bill suggested we start with $350 million but after eight years we had invested most of the $2 billion that I originally requested—and another $2 billion on scholarships.

The cochairs provided thoughtful leadership and gave me an extraordinary opportunity for which I will always be grateful. The two things I enjoyed most were the ability to travel every week and meet with the best educators in the world and the luxury of having conversations about how U.S. education could work differently and better, and have some ability to effect the desired change.

After my first year at the Gates Foundation, my oldest daughter graduated from a high school in the district where I was superintendent. After five years of sitting on the stage at high school graduations, I sat in the audience. As the students marched into the Tacoma Dome, it seemed as though there were not enough students in robes. I grabbed the program and counted—only four hundred. But I knew that we had sent six hundred students from two middle schools. I spent the next hour thinking about the two hundred students not on stage—nearly one-third of the students had not made it to graduation—and the thousands of students who had not graduated on my watch. I guess this should have been apparent from the annual budgets and enrollment projections that I submitted to the school board but it wasn't even discussed. This very personal learning experience, with subsequent confirmation of the national drop-out crisis by Chris Swanson (now at *Education Week*) and Jay Greene of the Manhattan Institute, led to my decade-long focus on improving U.S. high school graduation rates and college-preparation levels, particularly for low-income and minority students.

I have spent thirty years now in several major sectors of our economy, attempting to lead in business, nonprofit, public, and philanthropic organizations. I have some appreciation for the benefits and limitations of each sector. As the result of working with four hundred nonprofit education reform and advocacy organizations and with dozens of public school districts, it seems clear to me that we cannot achieve excellence and equity in education without the kind of innovation that only comes when private investment is involved. Producing innovations and taking them to scale is what private capital does best. Convinced that the world needed a dramatic increase in public and private learning investment, I cofounded Learn Capital, the only venture fund dedicated to learning. We invest in early-stage companies that provide innovative learning content, platforms, and services. The Learn Capital portfolio companies that are mentioned are noted in the list of companies and websites in the Appendix.

I advocate for and invest in learning entrepreneurs, *edupreneurs* as they've been called. I travel a lot. I visit schools around the world and meet with learning entrepreneurs and policy makers and blog about it every day at www.GettingSmart.com.

EXCELLENCE AND EQUITY

This book will make the case that innovation is key to excellence and equity in education; that learning is more important than ever; that it is easier, faster, and cheaper to do; and that personal digital learning is transforming formal education—and everything else.

I am convinced that there is an amazing new world of education right around the corner—engaging learning experiences for students, an exciting future for learning professionals, and productive options for families. This book is also a call to join me as an advocate for innovation in learning as the key to lifting the achievement of U.S. students and reaching the next billion young people worldwide.

READING THIS BOOK

This book was written for everyone who is a learner and specifically for people who care about elementary and secondary education. Following are a few words of advice for leaders, teachers, parents, learners, and investors.

EDUCATION LEADERS

It's time for you to put a stake in the ground. With pressure to achieve more with less, you know that your school(s) can't keep doing things the same old way. It's time to lead a conversation about the shift to personal digital learning: more engaged learning, extended learning time, and lifting the floor and blowing away the ceiling. People and politics will be more important than academics and technology during the transition. And you'll need to lead by example by being a digital learner yourself.

LEARNING PROFESSIONALS

Look around. There are so many new ways to teach. Technology is making the traditional job of teacher more manageable with engaging content and smart tools that allow you to network with students, provide access to excellent (and free) online tutorials, and offer a whole new generation of finely calibrated learning games. Many of these are described in Chapters Three to Five. As outlined in Chapter Nine, there are new jobs for teachers emerging: you can also teach online, start a school, or start a company. Similar to other professionals, you can work for yourself, create a partnership, or work in a public delivery system—the options are expanding; you can choose or create the work you love.

PARENTS

I hope that the material in this book—by revealing the breadth and complexity of the emerging online world—will help you want to explore it with your children and for your children. Of course, you know it's really up to you whether that time your child spends online is productive or not, and the more engaged you are the better. Fortunately the new learning software and online curriculum being introduced are more engaging and some of them allow you and your child's teacher to monitor activity. Also, as you'll see in Chapter Six, there is a new generation of schools that blend online and on-site learning in interesting ways, ways that might work well for your children.

LEARNERS (THAT'S ALL OF US)

There's a world of learning online—you can learn anything. There are a lot of choices online, many of them dumb, some dangerous. It's more important than ever for learners, young and old, to be self-managers and find the right balance between work and play (it's all the same to me). Set some goals, learn something new every day, week, month, and year. Write a blog; it's a great way to find out what you think you know.

INVESTORS

Whether you're seeking a return or just a big impact, the shift to personal digital learning is changing how schools work, how companies are run, and how the military trains the troops. I'll try to make the case in Chapter One that learning technology (tech) will be at least as important as clean tech and bio tech are to shaping the arc of human history. Edupreneurs are building curve-bending tools and schools that will improve the college and career preparation of millions of students around the world.

Let's get smart together.

ACKNOWLEDGMENTS

A lifetime of influences end up in a book. I'm grateful to the dozens of people who encouraged my work in education, the hundreds of people who helped shape my vision of what is possible, and the one hundred thousand teachers and leaders whom I've had the chance to work with, support, and learn from.

This book is primarily about what I think I've learned in the last few years working with smart partners at Learn Capital, supporting our portfolio companies, and serving on boards such as the International Association for K–12 Online Learning.

The discipline of daily blogging at www.GettingSmart.com continues to focus my learning. I appreciate dozens of thoughtful education bloggers, people who take the time to comment, and the more than one hundred people who agreed to be interviewed over the last two years.

Learning is a family affair. Karen, my partner of thirty-five years, supported my midcareer calling, persevered through a superintendency, continues to put up with constant travel, and runs our public affairs business. On top of challenging projects and busy schedules, our daughters, Caroline and Katherine, provided invaluable assistance by managing and supporting the process of writing this book. The whole family focused holiday and weekend attention on this project for over a year. I feel very fortunate to benefit from their love and support, their energy and enthusiasm, and their shared commitment to excellence and equity in education.

I appreciate the heroic leadership of Jeb Bush and Bob Wise, two former governors who have extended their national leadership as cochairs of *Digital Learning Now!,* a policy blueprint for the future of education.

I'm grateful for the people who read an early draft of this book and gave constructive criticism on how to make it better. Thanks to Kate Gagnon for suggesting the project, to Paula Stacey for editing my dense code, and for the support of the Jossey-Bass team.

ABOUT THE AUTHOR

Tom Vander Ark is CEO of Open Education Solutions, is a partner in Learn Capital, and blogs daily at www.GettingSmart .com.

Previously he served as president of the X PRIZE Foundation and was the executive director of education for the Bill & Melinda Gates Foundation. Tom was the first business executive to serve as public school superintendent. A prolific writer and speaker, Tom has published more than one thousand articles and blog posts. In December 2006, *Newsweek* readers voted Tom the most influential baby boomer in education.

Tom chairs the International Association for K–12 Online Learning (iNACOL) and serves on the board of AdvancePath Academics, LA's Promise, and Strive for College Collaborative.

Tom earned an engineering degree from Colorado School of Mines, which, in 2010, awarded him the Distinguished Achievement Medal. He received his MBA in finance from the University of Denver. He continues his education online.

GETTING SMART

HOW PERSONAL DIGITAL LEARNING WILL MAKE US SMART

If you saw three teens in the back of a classroom playing games, watching videos, and checking text messages, you would likely assume that little learning was going on. If you were in a classroom at most schools, you would be right. But there is another possibility. These students may be at one of a growing number of schools that are incorporating technology in exciting and productive ways. In fact, you could have observed the same three students in a coffee shop rather than a classroom and they may be deeply engaged in learning activities unlike any you have ever experienced. They may be part of a learning revolution that, with a little help from us, will be coming soon to a community (or a computer) near you.

Twenty years of prompting, investing, threatening, and reforming have largely failed to dramatically improve education in the United States. There may be pockets of excellence, but results from U.S. schools are flatlined. While unions and school boards argue about contract minutes, the rest of the developed world passed us by in achievement and high school graduation and college completion rates. The United States ranks near the bottom of developed countries in math, with nearly one-quarter of students unable to solve the easiest problems. More than 40 percent of students in Korea, Taiwan, and Singapore score at the advanced level in math and only 6 percent do in the United States.[2] The nation's 2009 report card indicated "that 38 percent of seniors demonstrated proficiency in reading and 26 percent reached that level in math. In addition, reading scores remain lower than they were in 1992. And the report found essentially no progress in closing achievement gaps that separate white students from black and Hispanic peers."[3]

The causes of our lagging performance are complicated but in short our schools are obsolete. They cannot accomplish what we need them to accomplish. Mass production style, our schools batch process each age group—some get it, others fail and repeat or drop out. We expect a lot out of teachers during the short school year but give them few tools to accomplish their complicated tasks. But there is a big opportunity right in front of us—to create schools that are engaging, are personalized, and work better for everyone. To better understand this opportunity let's take a closer look at that high school classroom described at the beginning of the chapter.

YES, THIS IS LEARNING

There's Maria, the girl checking text messages. Only these are not messages from friends or updates on a celebrity court appearance; they are responses from a local politician to her requests for interviews on immigration. As part of Maria's course on civics, she is deputy editor of a website attempting to illuminate the immigration debate. Maria has already interviewed a number of politicians and activists on both sides of the issue and has produced articles and opinion pieces judged by online peers and advisors. All of Maria's contributions are filed in an electronic portfolio. She is passionate about her work as an editor but she isn't quite as passionate about statistics. Later that day, she will go to her ninety-minute math lab, which combines self-paced online learning with occasional individualized online tutoring if she gets stuck. Even though she isn't excited about statistics and finds it difficult, this approach is working for her and she feels successful, unlike her experience in precalculus class last year in a traditional school environment, when she just couldn't learn at the same pace as the top students.

Eric is in front of a laptop, playing a game, but is this Angry Birds or World of Warcraft? No, it's an algebra game and as he views his score Eric sees that he's got more work to do on quadratics. His smart recommendation engine has already suggested a new math game that may provide a better learning mode for Eric—the system determined that his persistence improves under competitive situations with public recognition of his point status. Before trying out the new game, Eric takes a moment to check a discussion stream he is engaged in with his virtual learning team comparing two opposing views of tax policy. He notes that one of his teammates has cited a fact about the tax rates under Bill Clinton that he thinks may be wrong and when he checks his online source, he finds his instincts were right. He types a response with a correction.

Eric has completed enough units of study to complete lower division (what used to be the ninth and tenth grades). His culminating project and successful public demonstration will mark a midyear transition to upper division, when he will begin earning college credit and begin working on a career concentration including an internship.

Finally, we meet Isabel who is listening to her iPod and smiling. It isn't Kanye West or Lady Gaga who is making her smile, it is a lecture on Beethoven from McGill University that she had downloaded from iTunes U. Isabel is enrolled in the upper division of a virtual high school, she plays in a youth symphony, and music is her life. The lecture is only part of the background work she is doing in preparation for a project on music composition. Because Isabel does most of her learning at home, some folks are concerned about her lack of social interaction—in addition to her friends from the orchestra and soccer, she has a dozen mentors, is on five learning teams and four project teams, and regularly interacts with three academic advisors.

This isn't 2020 sci-fi. These portraits represent how millions of students could be learning with tools that are currently available to schools. Right now a small percentage of students in the United States are having these educational experiences. This is an emerging reality, a learning revolution under way, riding on the heels of the digital revolution, and rather than making us dumber, it has the power to help more students achieve academically and leave school prepared for work and further learning. It will extend learning to hundreds of millions of students. Personal digital learning can significantly boost traditional results. How this is happening and can happen are addressed in these pages. But before we return to the power of personal digital learning, let's look for a moment at the world that students will be learning and working in—an economy that is based increasingly on having good ideas.

IDEA ECONOMY

There are two growth economies in the United States—the idea economy and the service economy. Professional and technical jobs—the ideas jobs—are the ones that tend to be plugged into the global economy and that will continue to grow in number. At the other end of the pay scale are the services and helping professions including landscaper, waiter, cook, and health care aide. These jobs earn less than the median income—often minimum wage—and do not require a college degree; they are also expanding. The jobs that used to exist between these two sectors—the middle-class ones that created two-car-garage suburban America—are disappearing. MIT economist David Autor studied the disappearing act and concluded, "The structure of job opportunities in the United States has sharply polarized over the past two decades, with expanding job opportunities in both high-skill, high-wage occupations and low-skill, low-wage occupations, coupled with contracting opportunities in middle-wage, middle-skill white-collar and blue-collar jobs."[4]

The polarization of the economy is a big problem. As educators we can't fix the economy but what we can do is dedicate ourselves to making sure that as many students as possible are prepared to engage productively in the kinds of professional and technical jobs that that will help our economy and our students thrive. Learning is the entry ticket to the idea economy. "Most jobs that will have good prospects in the future will be complicated," says Louis Gerstner, former CEO of IBM. "They will involve being able to juggle data, symbols, computer programs in some way or the other."[5] But are our schools preparing students for this kind of work? I would say no. Let's look more closely at the features of the idea economy, at how ideas turn into industries, and compare them to the education we are currently providing.

JUST-IN-TIME LEARNING

The idea economy is iterative; it thrives on failure and feedback. By iterative I mean that ideas are tried and refined and tried again. It thrives on trial and error, risk and invention. Just listen to Marissa Mayer, Google's VP of Search: "We make mistakes every time, every day thousands of things go wrong with Google and its products that we know we can fix. But if you launch things and iterate really quickly, people forget about those mistakes and they have a lot of respect for how quickly you rolled the product out and made it better."[6]

Marissa's Google Search is both a product and driver of the idea economy. Search is a new form of idea economy learning: it is inquiry-based, iterative, and instantaneous. Search organizes the world's data to answer your questions: the better your question, the better the response. It is hard to imagine life before Internet searching—I don't know how we raised children, conducted business, or investigated illness without it. Google Search has turned us all into researchers, a shift whose importance we don't want to underestimate. Gisele Huff, executive director of the Jaquelin Hume Foundation, says, "The age of the expert is dead."[7] She points out that a doctor has hundreds of people and hundreds of ailments to worry about; you have one thing to worry about. If the doctor thinks you have adenoid cystic carcinoma, chances are you'll use a search engine to learn as much as you can about it. Search makes the world's knowledge accessible; now learning is just a matter of motivation and focus.

The just-in-time learning that Google enables is a far cry from the just-in-case learning our schools are now offering. Luckily, this economy—in which a compelling idea can become an industry—is beginning to also have an impact on education. Just look at Toby Rowland.

Late on Good Friday 2010 in London, Toby Rowland, CEO of start-up Mangahigh, was pleased at the number of high-level mathematics games played by students from all over the world—over twelve thousand on day one—with many from the United Kingdom where it was a national holiday. A self-described "geek" who loved school, Rowland worked at Walt Disney before launching King.com, the largest skills gaming company in the world. Toby realized that gaming was really luring kids into skills-based learning, whether they knew they were headed that way or not. Rowland recalls, "These people are improving their skills through casual games. If you made a different type of casual game, people could develop better skills that are much more valuable to them."[8]

Toby had a big idea: the same strategies that produce persistent game-play behavior could be used to teach students mathematics. Toby recruited top math experts and game designers and launched Mangahigh. By April 2010, Toby had seventy thousand young people around the world playing eight math games online. Toby's idea was enabled by the capacity and experience necessary to execute it. Mangahigh joins a handful of young companies that will transform learning from textbooks and tests to engaging and adaptive experiences.

Microsoft was created with the idea that computers could make us more productive. Google was created with the idea that search could be better. Walmart was created with the idea that retail could be more efficient. eBay was created with the idea that the web could be a marketplace. K^{12}, a $500 million e-learning giant, was created with the idea that schools could be conducted online. Each of these ideas attracted investment, created jobs, and launched an industry segment.

Having great ideas has long been a feature of the U.S. economy, a product of, among other things, a culture of independent thinking, financial markets, a venture-capital sector adept at taking ideas to scale, and a strong and diversified higher education system. But that could change if we don't nurture it. As Nayan Chanda, editor of YaleGlobal Online, wrote in an Indian publication, "The U.S. seems sadly unprepared to take advantage of the revolution it has spawned. The country's worn-out infrastructure, failing education system and lack of political consensus have prevented it from riding a new wave to prosperity."[9] When the bubble burst, the recession took more than wealth. "Americans are glum, dispirited and angry," Fareed Zakaria explained in *Time Magazine*. "The middle class, in particular, feels under assault. In a *Newsweek* poll in September, 63 percent of Americans said they did not think they would be able to maintain their current standard of living. Perhaps most troubling, Americans are strikingly fatalistic about their prospects. The can-do country is convinced that it can't."[10]

"CAN-DO" EDUCATION

I, for one, am very optimistic. Education has a profound role to play in how this country thinks about the future and the level of preparation its young people have for shaping it. We can innovate; I see it happening every week. Education reform got a big boost with the Obama administration's stimulus grant programs. But this book isn't about reform, it's about reinvention. If you extend a few trends and connect a few dots, you can imagine a system of public education with dramatically better results for the kids that need them most. We can shift from batch processing to personal digital learning but to do so means encouraging the entrepreneurs in our schools, embracing a new generation of learning tools, and inviting new providers to address unmet needs.

According to Gary Schoeniger, an entrepreneurship educator who writes for the Kauffman Foundation, "Entrepreneurs are fueled by their ideology and determined to make a difference. Armed with little more than a laptop and cell phone, fueled by their ideology, caffeine and a few credit cards, they set out against the status quo, breaking rules and blazing trails—redefining the world as they go." Ideally, this is the kind of energy we want to bring to our schools and have our students bring to their education and their work,

PREDICTIONS

In five years . . .

The Common Core State Standards and Race to the Top assessments will frame this decade of U.S education the way NCLB did the 2000s.

but as Schoeniger also observes, "The organizational mindset that we have so carefully cultivated—the mindset that fosters obedience, order and efficiency—may blind us to opportunity and hinder our ability to succeed in this new entrepreneurial economic environment."[11]

However, in *Customized Schooling*, Rick Hess and Olivia Meeks argue that it has been so hard for entrepreneurs to break into the school district–controlled system that "[t]he result is perverse, trapping educators and students in a ghetto where powerful new tools and services are curiosities rather than routine parts of the school day."[12]

The can-do education we need is starting to appear in a few spots from within but mostly from outside. The traditional system is being bypassed and redesigned by a learning revolution fueled by educational entrepreneurs who are creating new schools and new ways of learning, with personal digital learning at the core.

THE LEARNING REVOLUTION

Here is what this revolution looks like: customized learning is replacing a one-way slog through a print curriculum. Engaging media is motivating students to work harder and longer. Mobile technology is extending and expanding learning opportunities, especially for low-income students. Customization, motivation, and equalization will boost achievement, narrow gaps, and prepare more students for the idea economy. In these new educational environments, instead of annual feedback three months after the test, students can receive instant performance feedback and motivational reward mechanisms. District-run schools are being replaced by or are partnering with purpose-built learning networks: charter school chains such as KIPP (Knowledge Is Power Program) and franchise-like school developers with a common information platform, such as the New Tech Network.

What's driving this development? A confluence of forces over the last decade has begun to loosen the rigid hold that traditional approaches and structures have held on U.S. education; they include maturing information technology, the rise of informal learning opportunities, and a significant increase

TEN SHIFTS THAT CHANGE EVERYTHING

1. *Responsibility.* Families are taking back responsibility for learning, and choices in learning are exploding.
2. *Expectations.* These are shaping education in two ways. First, as the Common Core State Standards Initiative reveals, there is political consensus that all students should be eligible and prepared for higher education. Second, a generation that has grown up with the "my way" mindset expects more customization than a lecture hall can offer.
3. *Aspirations.* Rather than aspiring to having students achieve mastery that can be measured by standardized tests, schools need to focus on higher-order skills, such as the ability to create, perform, and persist under dynamic circumstances.
4. *Content.* Although there is value in curated content, textbook adoption is becoming an expensive relic. Education needs to look to everything from free online content to sophisticated learning programs with smart recommendation engines that suggest content based on learning level, interest, and best learning modality.
5. *Pedagogy.* Teacher-centered, lecture-based classrooms are giving way to student-centered, interactive, applied, and project-based learning. Master schedules will give way to interesting blends of customized learning experiences and projects that encourage integration and application. Just-in-time learning will become more common, slowly replacing the current model of just-in-case learning.
6. *Assessment.* The most important shift of the coming decade may be the instant feedback of assessment. As student learning shifts to a predominantly digital form, there will be a flood of keystroke data from games,

(continued)

simulations, virtual environments, end-of-unit quizzes, and adaptive assessments that will provide instant feedback to students and teachers.

7. *Grouping.* The model in which students of the same age slog through a print curriculum at the same rate is slowly giving way to individual progress models in which students learn at their own rate. Individual progress models—common in alternative education, online learning, and credit recovery—will become most prominent in high schools, community colleges, and certificate programs.

8. *Location.* Learning will take place anytime, anywhere. Students in high schools and colleges will increasingly assemble a transcript from multiple providers. Their formal certification may be place-based but their education will be unbounded.

9. *Culture.* Online, blended, and community-connected learning develops a mixed-age culture—old teaching young, young teaching old, and peer tutoring.

10. *Relationships.* Social networks will augment and then replace the classroom as the dominant organizing unit of learning. Although many students will matriculate at their own rate, they will do most of their learning as part of a virtual community.

in education philanthropy. Recently, the fiscal crisis made it impossible to continue usual operations. Together these forces are driving ten shifts in how education is and will be conducted.

In *Rethinking Education in the Age of Technology,* Collins and Halverson situated these shifts in a century of U.S. public education. The list above and the following table, adapted from their work, summarizes the shift from the one-room schoolhouse of the agrarian age to the giant suburban schools of the industrial age to the personal digital learning of the idea economy.

Agricultural to Industrial to Idea Economy Education[13]

Factor	From	To	To
Responsibility	Parents	State	Individuals and parents
Expectations	Social reproduction	Success for all	Individual choice
Aspirations	Practical skills	Discipline knowledge	Learning how to learn
Content	Books	Textbooks	Learning objects
Pedagogy	Apprenticeship	Didacticism	Interaction
Assessment	Observation	Testing	Embedded assessment
Grouping	Mixed-age	Age cohorts	Individual progress
Location	Home	School	Anywhere
Culture	Adult culture	Peer culture	Mixed-age culture
Relationships	Personal bonds	Authority figures	Social networks

CHARTER SCHOOLS

The coincidental birth in 1991 of the business-sponsored New American Schools Development Corporation, an effort to identify effective schoolwide restructuring models and charter school legislation beginning in Minnesota, ushered in a generation of almost ten thousand new schools. Many were developed in networks around an intentional school design and began sharing support services with similar schools around the country.

Typically authorized under a performance contract with a state, school district, or university to operate as an independent, public charter schools typically receive less funding than traditional schools and no funding for facilities. About a fifth of the more than five thousand charter schools in the United States are part of a managed network. More than three dozen high-performing charter school management organizations are revealing how responsive schools can be to students, teachers, and communities. Most networks aren't very innovative; they are just better managed than traditional schools—they hire talented people and help them execute at a high level every day. Execution across the managed networks is aided by perpetual rather than political leadership—the (mostly nonprofit) boards are appointed to support an organizational mission rather than elected to serve a political agenda, as is often the case on public school boards.

Consider some of the school networks that think hard about preparing kids for their future and not our past. Expeditionary Learning, which draws on Outward Bound principles, is based, in part, on "the having of wonderful ideas."[14] It is precisely this notion of rewarded curiosity that is essential for a leader in the idea economy. Charter school networks such as High Tech High in San Diego, Envision Schools in San Francisco, and Denver School of Science and Technology bring learning to life with deep explorations and public demonstrations.

Evidence of what the Hewlett Foundation calls deeper learning can be seen in student work at these schools—papers written, books published, videos produced, artwork created—and even more compelling is the sparkle of confidence in students' eyes when asked to describe work they know is of professional quality.

Some independent charter schools struggle academically, should not have been authorized in the first place, and should be closed. Remember the iterative process that brought us Google Search? As charter schools try, fail, learn from each other, and succeed, they are bringing important lessons about efficient and responsive management to education. A few are showing us exciting things about how students can learn differently, the importance of feedback loops, a culture of achievement, and the benefits (and shortcomings) of performance contracting— all things that are paving the way for a new future of learning.

Charter schools, and charter management organizations in particular, were among the most important developments of the last decade. However, they only serve about 3 percent of U.S. students and still require a lot of charity to operate and grow. It's time to take the lessons learned and the effective models developed over the last decade and supercharge them with technology.

THE TECHNOLOGY

If you need to learn how to calculate the slope of a line, a quick Internet search will yield a Wikipedia explanation, a Khan Academy tutorial, a couple of learning games, several peer-to-peer learning sites, and lots of YouTube videos. The notion of a textbook as just one way to learn is suddenly very antiquated.

New digital tools are also fueling the current learning revolution. Computer learning games, discussed in more depth in Chapter Four, that are based on the neuropsychology of learning and motivation have the potential to engage students in ways we had never thought possible. We are likely to learn far more than we know in the coming decade about finding the "hook" that will improve persistence through difficult work. We are experimenting with how to finely access student learning and student learning styles based on keystroke data that are tracked and analyzed from computer learning programs. In fact, we are on the verge of creating and putting to use psychological understandings of student profiles that indicate, for example, when a student prefers competition to collaboration, works harder if public recognition is involved, and is most persistent between 10 PM and 1 AM. As you will see in the following chapters, we are getting a lot smarter about getting smart.

We are living through the historic shift from getting our information from print to digital forms. The technology revolution transformed business and entertainment and will have an equally profound impact on learning. Now that anyone can learn nearly anything nearly anywhere for free or cheap, all bets are off. The learning race, not the arms race, will define the future. This book is about our future, about the power of digital learning to help us finally reach and teach all students, no matter their neurological profile, geographical position, or socioeconomic background. And so, I'd like to conclude here with an inspiring and exciting story that points to the future of learning, a future in which technology can be harnessed to provide exciting opportunities for students in hard-to-reach places.

Ushodaya High occupies the dark and crowded upper floors of a dated retail strip under the shadow of the elevated airport expressway in a forgotten slum south of Hyderabad.

PREDICTIONS

In five years . . .

Low-cost blended private schools will serve close to two hundred million students in India, China, and Africa. More than half will use low-cost mobile learning technology.

16

The expressway speeds passengers from a modern airport to a bustling information technology downtown in south central India. Many students in India don't have access to quality public schools, particularly those in urban slums. Ushodaya students were lucky to find this low-cost private school run by Praveen Kumar, and Praveen was lucky to have been discovered by Neera Nundy. Born in Canada, Neera attended Harvard Business School and decided to move back to India to help bottom-of-the-pyramid entrepreneurs such as Praveen unleash their ideas. Neera and her husband launched Dasra, a grant-funded social enterprise that supports dozens of social entrepreneurs every year. One of the 2009 recipients included Praveen. With Neera's help, Praveen improved teacher pay and support, began keeping financial statements, and is connecting more slum kids with college and career opportunities in the idea economy. In a couple years, Praveen will be able to add online learning using low-cost tablet computers and free curriculum. He'll be able to leverage good teachers and reach a few more of the half-billion Indian young people eager to get smart.

With demand created by the idea economy, the learning revolution is being fueled by expanding access to broadband, cheap mobile devices, and powerful new tools. It is increasingly possible for anyone to learn anything almost anywhere. That allows us (and forces us) to reinvent the delivery of public education. So let's get started.

AMERICAN EDUCATION

New Students in an Old System

My youngest daughter (and blog editor) Katie went to kindergarten in 1994, the year the Internet became a global phenomenon. She attended a new school with lots of computers and had access to several at home. She doesn't remember life without the web, chat, cell phone, or downloadable music. In second grade, Mrs. Knoll had her playing computer math games at school. In fifth grade her summer assignments included PowerPoint presentations on the Impressionists.

By seventh grade, homework was multitasked with Napster downloads, AIM chats, and TV. Before she went to college in 2008, she had Facebooked most of her dorm. When I asked the college president what he thought about the first class to come to campus fully networked, he asked me, "What's Facebook?" Other than a couple traditional high school and college courses, all of her learning experiences have been a blend of digital and hands on. Katie configures our printers, sets up our TV remotes, and finds us smart phone applications (apps). Katie grew up learning online and the adults around her run to catch up.

Although not all students grew up with the same opportunities, most students grow up digital to some degree or another. Their lives have been shaped by a digital culture that allows them to interact with the world and with each other in ways that the adults who are teaching them and parenting them can only try to imagine. They are bringing a whole new set of skills and expectations to their schooling and their work lives; unfortunately, instead of valuing and building on these skills, many in education look at students' engagement with information and social networking technology with reactions ranging from disdain to downright horror. Think about it. How did you respond when you read the description of Katie's multitasking homework sessions at age twelve? Wonder what kind of parent would let a seventh-grader have free access

---

PREDICTIONS

In ten years . . .

Most U.S. students will attend a blended school where students report to a physical space and most learning happens online.

---

to a computer? Think that she was on the road to ruin? She finished high school *and* college in five years and now blogs about digital learning. Katie, a digital native, isn't successful in spite of her engagement with technology. She is successful because of it.

Digital native is a term coined by Don Tapscott, author of *Growing Up Digital* and *Wikinomics,* to describe those who grew connected to the virtual world and everything it has to offer—relationships, music, news, entertainment, and sophisticated gaming.[1] John Palfrey and Urs Gasser, authors of *Born Digital,* summarize how different this generation is:

> There is one thing you know for sure: These kids are different. They study, work, write, and interact with each other in ways that are very different from the ways that you did growing up. They read blogs rather than newspapers. They often meet each other online before they meet in person. They probably don't even know what a library card looks like, much less have one; and if they do, they've probably never used it. They get their music online—often for free, illegally—rather than buying it in record stores. They're more likely to send an instant message (IM) than to pick up the telephone to arrange a date later in the afternoon. They adopt and pal around with virtual Neopets online instead of pound puppies. And they're connected to one another by a common culture. Major aspects of their lives—social interactions, friendships, civic activities—are mediated by digital technologies. And they've never known any other way of life.[2]

According to a $50 million exploration in youth media funded by the John D. and Catherine T. MacArthur Foundation, *Living and Learning with New Media,* "America's youth are developing important social and technical skills online—often in ways adults do not understand or value."[3] Key findings included the following:

- Youth understand the social value of online activity and are generally highly motivated to participate.

- Young people are learning basic social and technical skills that they need to fully participate in contemporary society.

- The social worlds that youth are negotiating have new kinds of dynamics because online socializing is permanent, is public, involves managing elaborate networks of friends and acquaintances, and is always turned on.

- The Internet provides new kinds of public spaces for youth to interact and receive feedback from one another.

- Young people respect each other's authority online and are more motivated to learn from each other than from adults.

- Most youth are not taking full advantage of the learning opportunities of the Internet.

This last bullet is critical. Students may be digital natives and are primed and ready to learn online but they can't do this on their own. They need the schools to support, rather than judge and push against, the skills and expectations they bring to their learning. As Marc Prensky, author of *Digital Game-Based Learning,* explains, "Students certainly don't have short attention spans for their games, movies, music, or Internet surfing. More and more, they just don't tolerate the old ways—and they are enraged that we are not doing better by them."[4]

ENEMY NUMBER ONE: BOREDOM

When you visit high schools, it's striking to note the difference in affect and energy between hallways and classrooms. Young people have developed a "power-down" feature that is activated when they enter a class. Boredom may be the greatest challenge we face. Of course, boredom has always been a feature of schools. We've all experienced it to greater and lesser degrees. There's the boredom of slogging through all of the down time, while teachers take role, while we file into assemblies, or while we wait and wait for something to happen that relates to us and what we are learning. Then there's the boredom of listening to a teacher lecture about something completely irrelevant or explain something for the second, third, or fourth time. And finally, there's the boredom of listening to a teacher, yet again, chastise the same student for the same behavior.

PREDICTIONS

In five years . . .

Science will confirm the obvious about how most boys learn and active learning models will be developed in response using expeditions, playlists, and projects.

Yes, we accept this as a feature of our schools, but why? Because it's what we experienced as students? At the best schools, public and private, the educational experience is more challenging and more personalized—students are asked to think.

Defenders of liberal arts education have always emphasized critical thinking. The Association of American Colleges and Universities summarizes it elegantly:

> Liberal Education is an approach to learning that empowers individuals and prepares them to deal with complexity, diversity, and change. It provides students with broad knowledge of the wider world (e.g., science, culture, and society) as well as in-depth study in a specific area of interest.[5]

It is hard to argue with those aspirations. The opportunity for students to make occasional in-depth studies in an area of interest is an important luxury; it mirrors what most of them will do for the rest of their lives—research, synthesize, demonstrate, and advocate. Proponents of liberal education make rational arguments about the importance of content and discipline knowledge. E. D. Hirsch, author of *Cultural Literacy* and *The Knowledge Deficit,* argues for a traditional, "knowledge-oriented" academic approach with rich, factual content.[6] Combined with the U.S. preoccupation with standardized tests, advocates for covering more material have, in a perverse way, *reduced* the amount of critical thinking in U.S. schools rather than making it more widespread. Liberal education has the right inclination toward critical thinking and its application. But this isn't what students are getting in our schools. Mile-wide, inch-deep state standards and multiple-choice testing have subverted the liberal education intent and left us with a boring, less useful, and less relevant set of expectations.

LOOKING BACK, LOOKING FORWARD

In shaping schools for new students entering a new world, we have to look backward and forward: back to the liberal tradition that emphasizes deep exploration and critical thinking and forward to a digital future that will allow us to make such an education available to all students.

Cincinnati-based operating foundation KnowledgeWorks, led for a decade by Chad Wick, a former bank CEO passionate about connecting urban kids to the idea economy, developed a 2020 forecast that outlines five new learning priorities:[7]

1. Students need the ability to sort, verify, synthesize, and use information to make judgments and take action. These skills have always been important but now that we're all drinking from a fire hose of information they are essential.

2. Students need a working knowledge of market economics and personal finance—most students still leave high school without one. Students will be navigating an increasingly dynamic economy in which technologies will improve and change at exponential rates and market opportunities will be big but competitive. Students need the ability to sell—themselves and an idea. They need to experience and give candid performance feedback and gain appreciation for a quality work product.

   Curtis Carlson, the chief executive of SRI International, an independent research institute, told Tom Friedman, "Fortunately, this is *the best time ever* for innovation." Carlson gave three reasons: "First, although competition is increasingly intense, our global economy opens up huge new market opportunities. Second, most technologies—since they are increasingly based on ideas and bits and not on atoms and muscle—are improving at rapid, exponential rates. And third, these two forces—huge, competitive markets and rapid technological change—are opening up one major new opportunity after another."[8]

3. Students need to be able to gather evidence and construct an argument. In an electronic democracy, where issues will be argued less in mainstream media such as newspapers and cable news and more through social media, students need to learn how to critique and make arguments in ways they have never before been called on to do (for example, a 140-character Twitter defense).

   Most young people will work in diverse teams in which forming temporary agreements is fundamental to getting stuff done. They will more frequently be asked to draw inference from complex text. Young people are more likely than ever to enter complex situations in their personal and professional lives when they are asked to hold competing ideas in tension and make quick judgments.

4. Students need sophisticated communication skills across a variety of media. Video and mixed media will continue to grow in importance but writing will remain vitally important. They will face a world with more ways to make a living than ever before, requiring frequent interaction with people from different parts of the world, with different levels of education, and with different work habits. The emotional intelligence to read people and situations across multiple cultures will be ever more critical, from the service counter attendant to the CEO.

5. The dynamic economy demands that we take charge of our own learning, figure out what we need to learn, and find or create a way to learn it. Consumer choice is expanding in nearly every aspect of life: retail, music, religion, communications, entertainment, and education. Going to the grocery store or turning on the TV involves many more choices than a generation ago. Choice proliferation makes

personal management, decision making, and the ability to judge the veracity of information sources essential skills.

The following table summarizes these learning priorities and the five information economy trends that are fueling them. They form a set of new basic skills that should be a priority for every K–12 student and school.

Five Information Economy Implications[9]

Trend	Idea Economy Preparation
Information proliferation	Ability to verify information, recognize patterns, analyze data sets, and synthesize
Dynamic economy	Understanding of free enterprise and personal finance; appreciation of and ability to produce quality work products
Electronic democracy	Success in making and critiquing an argument, participating on a diverse team, and dealing with paradox
Connected organizations and lives	Ability to communicate in a variety of media, to participate in networks, and to navigate distributed organizations
Choice proliferation	Track record of personal management and initiative demonstrating independent work and judgment

THE POWER OF PERSONAL DIGITAL LEARNING

Clearly, digital technology is playing a large role in shaping these new learning priorities. So, it is fitting that we would look to digital technology to help us craft an approach to education that will allow us to fulfill these learning priorities. But my central thesis—that personal digital learning will make us smarter—is not simply based on the idea that a digital economy in a digital world requires a digital education. Although this may ultimately be true, it is essential that we understand exactly what digital learning will allow us to do. What makes it powerful? How will we change the way students learn? How does it build on ways students are already primed and ready to learn?

Let's look back again for a moment at the liberal arts tradition of great schools, which provide the following:

- *Customization.* A curriculum and pedagogy that respond to the strengths, weaknesses, and interests of those who attend

- *Motivation.* Approaches that make learning fun, interesting, challenging, and meaningful

- *Equalization.* The best teachers, books, materials, and tools, even access to other excited and motivated students

As I describe in the following chapters, this is what digital learning can provide. In fact, if we revisit now the profile of the digital natives described at the beginning of this chapter, we can see that the digital world they inhabit is offering them exactly these three powerful features. They are used to customizing their own devices, sites, and learning experiences— seeking out what interests them and finding help online where and when they need it. They are also used to playing intricate and complex games on computers, based on sophisticated software that knows how to calibrate new challenges to the player's past successes and failure, one of the essential keys to motivating learners. Finally, they have access, 24/7, to the best of everything—whether it be friends, family, or expertise. Our kids are ready for new learning options: one-to-one mobile access, personalized content, virtual environments, social networks, big questions, and engaging applications. They are ready to learn at home, on the job, in the community, as well as at school. The question is, are we ready to create the schools our students deserve?

CUSTOMIZATION

Building the Right Playlist for Each Student

Anyone who has been on an airplane, sat in an airport, or spent time on a bus, in a café, or even in traffic knows that the workplace is no longer a place and the workday is no longer an expanse of time. Work happens everywhere now. I can participate in conference calls while I'm walking on the beach, review reports and write memos at thirty thousand feet, and get back to people on the East Coast at midnight so they'll have answers to pressing questions before I wake up the next day.

The technology that makes this all possible is getting cheaper and is available to almost everyone. People who even three years ago might have wondered what a BlackBerry was and why anyone would want one are now reading books on Kindles or watching movies on an iPad. They are researching family trees, setting up Facebook pages, and connecting with family via Skype. They filter the world of news and blogs on a customized iGoogle page. And they are playing games—on their phone, on their tablet, on their TV. They are joining online communities, engaging in political activism via the Internet, and educating themselves on anything and everything, all when and where it works for them.

It is no surprise: technology has allowed us to customize our worlds to suit our needs, interests, and situations. Although people may sigh and whine a bit about how overwhelming it all is—clearly, we are still adapting—who among us would go back to the way it was fifteen, ten, even two years ago?

A scary brave new world or just a great new way to live? The question is academic because, of course, we aren't going to go back. But for those who fear that giving over education to this world means relinquishing our last hold on quality and the focused brain, it is important to challenge the assumption that focus, deep learning, and even social connections depend on students spending six hours at a desk in school.

What is the ideal education model? Technology may put an end to that debate because the answer will increasingly be "whatever works best for that student." We need to build on children's strengths, leverage exploration of their interests, shore up in areas where they are weak, and graduate them with a personalized plan. In other words, we need to customize.

DIFFERENTIATION

Educators know that it is a ridiculous fallacy to assume that all children learn in the same way and at the same rate, but that's how our system is organized. Administrators encourage differentiated instruction in classrooms—a noble idea, but similar to many of the reforms and pedagogical advances that we try to implement in our schools, it is doomed to fail. This isn't to say that some students won't benefit from the heroic and inventive efforts of certain teachers who are trained and practiced in the art of differentiation, but the overall impact is limited.

Strategies for differentiation range from thematic units leveled for individual students, to presenting the same material to the whole class using different modes (visual, auditory, kinesthetic) to reach different "learning styles," to grouping students according to ability and shaping lessons for each group. Proponents of differentiation urge teachers to provide a good balance between teacher-selected and student-selected tasks with the idea that students should be allowed to find their own level and pursue their own interests—to customize whenever possible. But how possible is this in a classroom of twenty-five to thirty students (or 150 at the secondary level), each bringing his and her own set of emotional and cognitive strengths and weaknesses to the room for the day? A single teacher, no matter how effective, is limited by the constraints imposed on her by the traditional school structure.

PREDICTIONS

In ten years . . .

With a decade of data, second-generation recommendation engines will drive tutoring applications that are more effective than one-on-one sessions with a live tutor.

Paul Wezman, who was on the planning team for Enterprise Elementary, a school that opened in the district between Seattle and Tacoma where I was superintendent in 1994—the year the Internet exploded—is an example of a teacher who began to find a way to differentiate through technology. He pushed hard for lots of computers and got enough for teams of two students to share one. Paul was one of the few people who quickly understood the implications of the Internet. Rather than fighting over the four library books on Egypt, the students could cruise archives in Cairo. He customized the class for every fifth- and sixth-grade student and then let them fly. Students stifled by a traditional classroom were challenged to move ahead and to tutor classmates. For younger and struggling students, Paul differentiated the degree of difficulty. In the self-directed classroom, Paul helped each student set goals and tailor the focus of projects. Instead of insisting that they demonstrate learning only through writing, Paul let them demonstrate their learning in different ways including videos, presentations, and visual displays.

Good teachers like Paul have always differentiated instruction for learners at different levels. They've looked for ways to motivate individual students and they've tried to apply and extend learning. But what made the difference wasn't just Paul's commitment to reaching and teaching each student, it was his vision and willingness to draw on instructional technology to make each student a self-directed learner, to leverage strengths and interests, and to address specific needs.

INDIVIDUAL PROGRESS

There are thousands of schools that use technology schoolwide to support an individual progress model in which demonstrated mastery rather than birthdays and semesters mark transitions. Many of these schools are finding ways to customize learning through technology and are helping students not well served by the traditional system. Performance learning centers (PLCs), created by Communities In Schools (a national nonprofit that connects students to mentors and support services), is a network of drop-out prevention academies serving overaged and undercredited students. Like with AdvancePath (profiled in Chapter Six), PLC students select online courses and work at their own pace with the support of on-site teachers who provide on-demand and small-group tutoring. Students who are behind can earn credits at an accelerated rate and graduate on time. Thousands of school districts now offer credit-recovery options online, some with the kind of focused support common at a PLC.

Personal digital learning is competency-based and focuses not on hours spent but on what students learn and can demonstrate. A report by iNACOL (International Association for K–12 Online Learning) clarifies the features of competency-based learning: (1) students advance on mastery, (2) it provides explicit and measurable learning objectives that empower students, and (3) assessment is meaningful and a positive learning experience for students. (The report points out how crazy the idea of failing and repeating a grade is when some students just need a little extra time and a different way to learn.)[1]

HAVE IT YOUR WAY

For fifteen years starting in 1995 the first generation of online learning was used primarily to vary rate, time, and location but still required a one-way slog though a body of content. A new generation of Web 2.0 learning tools, based on the same technology that allows us to customize our lives, allows us now to completely rethink learning. Instead of starting with the institution, we can start with students and can customize a sequence of learning experiences to suit their needs and interests. With the explosion of instructional content, it is becoming easier for students (or teachers or smart engines) to choose the most effective instructional modality: recorded tutorials (Khan Academy), live tutoring (tutor.com), short videos (BrightStorm), games (Mangahigh), lectures (Academic Earth), text with voiceover (HippoCampus), or free online textbooks (CK-12). Social learning platforms such as Edmodo—a Facebook for schools—make it easy for teachers to drop personalized assignments into a chat stream. Similarly, higher education social tools such as GoingOn turn courseware into community conversations and online Socratic seminars. As learning games (discussed in Chapter Four) become part of every day, it will be easy for students to "skin" (personalize the appearance the way you scribbled on a book cover) a virtual environment and to set their preference for best interpersonal modalities: collaboration, competition, individual exploration, or team-based challenges.

In addition to these high-tech strategies, schools that blend online and on-site learning can vary locations. Families can travel together more often. With portable education, schools and students can take more advantage of community assets such as museums, theaters, and natural resources. Schools like the ones supported by Big Picture Learning customize internships for every student. Projects and science fairs allow students to customize around interests. The point of all this customization is to boost engagement, persistence, achievement, and completion rates.

INSTANT FEEDBACK

Customized learning will be driven by the instant feedback of content-embedded assessment. As student learning shifts to a predominantly digital mode, the data gained can be used to create individual learning plans. The ability to customize learning and the knowledge to be gained about students will make this the most important development of the decade.

Here is a snapshot of a portion of data collected from one day from students in school environments that incorporate next-generation components rich with feedback.

Data from a Five-Thousand-Keystroke Fifth-Grade Student Day

- *Reading:* An hour of reading was initiated with an adaptive quiz that checked reading level and adjusted content; the session was concluded with a comprehension quiz. The three-hundred keystrokes resulted in two entries in a standards-based gradebook—evidence that the student had met two standards.

- *Math games:* Two different adaptive games played for twenty minutes each produced 1,400 keystrokes, which allowed programs to adjust difficulty and pacing and yielded analyses rich with data on the student's persistence.

- *Writing:* Three writing prompts resulted in four hundred words of output but the editing process captured three thousand keystrokes that can tell the teacher about how the answers were constructed (and easily detect if they were cut and pasted).

Data from a Ten-Thousand-Keystroke Tenth-Grade Student Day

- *Writing:* A project management tool encouraged production of a five-hundred-word opinion piece as part of a thematic unit. The editing process captured six thousand keystrokes and a list of all the sites that were accessed to produce the piece.

- *Guidance:* The online advisory system suggested three short videos on careers related to the thematic writing project and based on indicated interests. It also suggested a vocabulary builder to boost SAT scores.

- *Physics:* Fifty minutes on two simulations yielded 1,400 keystrokes that resulted in a score, a record of the student's pathway, and some information about preferences.

- *Math:* Exercises at the end of three-minute tutorials yielded two hundred keystrokes and a score entered in a standards-based gradebook.

- *Chinese:* A fifty-minute immersive social learning session with Chinese speakers and other novices yielded two hundred mouse clicks and a progress report, and suggested a smart phone vocabulary game.

- *Music:* About two thousand clicks during a sixty-minute music composition session resulted in a three-minute video and a record of interests, skills, and knowledge of music theory.

Even though a growing number of schools capture student achievement data in a learning management system, none of the current systems contemplate a ten-thousand-keystroke data set—but, for millions of students, it's already here.

LEARNER PROFILES

Smart learner profiles will guide learning and be central to educational architecture (virtual and physical) in the future. Profiles will include learning levels, interests, best learning modalities, and portfolios rich with artifacts of learning. Capturing more data on more dimensions will allow systems to make smart recommendations for students—key to customized learning.

Comprehensive profiles will enable students to bring an enormously useful and rich amount of information to every new educational environment they enter. Conversely, a digitally generated profile can easily gather information from a range of environments, such as from after-school and summer-school providers, tutoring and test-prep organizations, and informal learning applications. Here's what that might look like: when students sign in to a parent-paid online tutoring session, they would be queried about connecting with their profile; the connection not only would guide tutoring initiation but also would contribute to an evolving and data-rich profile of each student as a learner.

Of course, such profiles raise privacy concerns, which could prove to be a big barrier to rich customized learning if they aren't addressed up front. Fortunately, the technology exists to deal with these concerns. A unique student identifier, for example, now available in most states, provides confidentiality and portability. Giving families the ability to manage privacy with a Facebook-like privacy profile would help them decide what information they want to share with whom.

SMART ENGINES

Amazon knows what you want to read next; iTunes can predict your music taste; Netflix will suggest a movie you'll enjoy. These sites analyze your purchasing behaviors and those of people like you to make purchase recommendations. They have helped to build customer loyalty and drive sales. In education, smart recommendation engines will be the "killer app" (a functionality that leads to breakthrough performance). Recommendation engines will become central to curriculum development and lesson planning; they will help sort, rate, and suggest the right lesson at the right time for every student.

Math programs like DreamBox, aimed at the K–3 grades, and Mangahigh, a game-based prealgebra product, suggest content of just the right level of difficulty to help students stay motivated. At the collegiate level, Arizona State announced a personalized learning partnership with the test-prep platform Knewton to improve their developmental (that is, remedial) math sequence. "Knewton has demonstrated results with their test-prep products and we were excited about the possibilities of bringing this to larger scale education classroom settings," said Phil Regier, dean of ASU Online. "This will show how adaptive learning technology and organic engagement drive better learning outcomes and higher graduation rates."[2] By organic, Regier means on students' own terms, when and where they want help. These simple recommendation engines just define the student's learning level and dish up lessons that are just the right level of difficulty. They run against a small private library of lessons.

PREDICTIONS

In five years . . .

Most learning platforms will feature a smart recommendation engine, similar to iTunes Genius, that will build recommended learning experiences for students.

Smart recommendations that drive learning playlists will be far more sophisticated than these early examples I described previously. In addition to learning levels, smart engines will base recommendations on a student's interests and the learning modality that has been most successful for him. School of

One (see Chapter Six for a more detailed profile), the award-winning, innovative New York City math program, has an algorithm that suggests lessons based on the prior day's performance, self-reported interests, and best learning mode (initially based on a pretest, which is adjusted based on performance). By 2011, the School of One instructional database included thousands of lessons. Future recommendation engines will crawl the web in search of learning content considering millions of options and hundreds of student variables to identify the best possible next learning experience.

The education debate in the United States is preoccupied with school choice but technology is pushing choice to the course and lesson level. The focus is shifting from institutions to individuals. In a digital learning environment, personalization at the lesson level can be a choice between small-group instruction, online tutoring, a simulation, or a learning game. It will increasingly include a choice of providers: local school, district program, statewide provider (for example, Florida Virtual School), and national provider (for example, K^{12} and Connections Academy).

By 2015, there will be several school networks that blend playlists and projects to customize learning. Playlists of skill-building exercises and experiences available anytime, anywhere on inexpensive tablets will prepare students to participate in team-based interdisciplinary explorations that attack big questions, demand critical thinking, and require extensive writing, and culminate with a public presentation.

PERSONALIZED GUIDANCE

Good schools personalize learning by making sure every student feels known and respected. An advisory structure provides frequent points of contact and support. It usually includes a couple periods of contact between an advisor and a group of about twenty students. Over the course of several years, a good advisor can change the trajectory of a young person's life, but it's hard work with little support. In the next few years, online guidance systems will begin supporting six or seven key functions:

- Providing an overview of academic progress that will inform course-taking decisions

- Building study skills and personal management competencies (the "how to succeed in school" skills that are assumed but never taught)

- Promoting career awareness and identifying job exposure opportunities (job shadows and internships)

- Monitoring social and emotional health and supporting connections to youth and family services

- Building a learning transcript that includes evidence of learning and a portfolio of work accumulated inside and outside formal education environments

- Providing a support system that will help students and families make the best possible postsecondary decision— an eHarmony for college

- Making connections through a LinkedIn-like learner profile that will share portions of the learner transcript and work experiences with a web of people who can help, including mentors, institutions of further and higher education, and prospective employers

These online guidance systems won't replace the important role of sustained adult relationships but they will support student decision making and guide and extend the work of mentors and advisors.

PLATFORM ECOSYSTEMS

Customized learning will be enabled by cloud-based learning services (applications on remote servers that allow you to use what you want, when you want, where you want, on any device) with lots of applications and vendors offering support services. These digital services will replace today's learning management systems that run boring online courses that aren't much better than electronic textbooks. As we're already seeing on iPhone and Android, platform services will unleash development of learning applications that will motivate and improve learning. Next-generation learning services will include lots of engaging content and social networking features—learning will be more like spending time on Facebook and YouTube than reading a textbook. A rich array of applications will support learners and teachers. Teachers will be aided by individualized recommendations based on tons of keystroke data. A community of vendors will provide aligned services including student tutoring, staff development, school improvement, and new school development. This type of platform opportunity is what drove Rupert Murdoch to hire former New York City chancellor Joel Klein and buy Wireless Generation.

MERIT BADGES

When it comes to customized learning the Scouts got it right. For one hundred years they have been awarding badges for Scouts who show what they know. There are three great pedagogical techniques incorporated into the system: (1) Scouts pick the badges they want to work on, (2) they pick a counselor who has special knowledge in the area to serve as a

(continued)

guide and proctor, and (3) they demonstrate their knowledge in some required ways and in some self-selected ways.

Taking the best from the Boy Scouts and Foursquare (a site that makes a game of daily activities and awards badges) a merit badge system would provide a visual pathway for learning and a motivational reward system. Each badge would consist of a set of competency clusters with mastery demonstrated in several ways, perhaps one machine scored and one teacher scored. Like Boy Scout badges, each would have some compulsory components and some components that individual students can customize. Also like Boy Scout badges, connecting with an external expert would provide mentoring, application opportunities, and another demanding source of performance feedback. The requirements for a badge on fractions could include the option of several learning games, a video tutorial with sample problems, a project, and a quiz. A traditional text explanation could be included (mostly for parents). The badge would be awarded based on the combination of game and quiz scores and the graded project. What makes this unit of instruction interesting is that students can choose when to work on it, how long to spend on it, and how to approach the experience; and they receive a badge for their virtual sash when completed. We can begin to imagine a DIY (do-it-yourself) high school with a sequence of badges so engaging and a path so intuitive that some students can almost do it themselves. Many of the badges would provide for interaction with subject matter experts (teachers and community members) but students would be able to take ownership of their own learning. Compared to the infantilization of eighteen-year-olds that occurs in high school today, a badge approach could lead to a generation of schools that are each a series of engaging learning experiences rather than what seems like a string of boring classes.

As we will see in Chapter Six on model schools, customized learning is beginning to happen not just in the United States but throughout the world. It is not limited to formal education but is proliferating in informal learning experiences on test-prep sites, peer-to-peer sites, and free and pay learning game sites. We're about to experience the power and productivity of the "school of one."

MOTIVATION

Getting Everyone in the Learning Game

Motivation, the holy grail of education, is so important and so elusive, and yet we know very little about it. In the nascent field of cognitive sciences, hypotheses about learning styles have drawn a good deal of attention from researchers and educators, leaving more fundamental questions of motivation underexplored. Because we need kids to work hard, we need a much more sophisticated and individualized sense of what will capture students' attention and cause them to persist through discomfort and distraction. Our ability to quickly and efficiently get and use a deep understanding of the intrinsic and extrinsic factors that together cause focused and persistent behavior in each student—a personal motivational profile—will fundamentally change education and the learning professions.

We are seeing exciting breakthroughs that are getting us very close to this ideal. Who do we have to thank for this? Any thirteen-year-old could tell you the answer. It's game designers. We can learn a lot about persevering behaviors by observing the casual game space. Different games attract different players. Some prefer combat over collaboration, some realism over alternative realities, some a race over exploration. Nearly all games provide instant performance feedback. Perhaps most important, most games offer the benefit of public victories and private failures—both important to most kids.

Let's consider what those who design and study games have to say.

PREDICTIONS

In five years . . .

Information from keystroke data will unlock the new field of motivation research, yielding insights about what causes students to persist through difficult work.

ON THE VERGE OF AN EPIC WIN

Jane McGonigal is a designer of alternative reality games who thinks that games have the motivational power to help us change the world and has written a book about it, *Reality Is Broken: Why Games Make Us Better and How They Can Change the World*. But the alternative reality games that she designs aren't making billions of dollars for game manufacturers; they are truly designed in conjunction with nonprofits, challenging people to come together to solve problems such as poverty, hunger, and climate change.

One of her best-known games is EVOKE, which she designed for the World Bank Institute, to help educate and inspire young people across the world, and in particular in Africa, to find ways to work for social innovation. A bit of background: the idea grew out of a continental conference organized by Robert Hawkins of the World Bank Institute on the education and knowledge economy in Africa. In dialogue with African universities it was clear that there was little community outreach and no history of social entrepreneurship. The universities wanted an information-sharing platform to help spread good ideas but Robert decided that it might be more effective to develop an alternative reality game that would resonate with students. The game officially began in March 2010 and when it ended (people can still play, but the first game is officially over), according to Hawkins's blog post on the World Bank website, over 19,324 people from more than 150 countries registered to play.[1] In the first month of play, EVOKE generated close to 10 percent of the page views of the entire World Bank external website. A review of the game and its effects reveals, among other things, that EVOKE encouraged people to go into their communities, bring back ideas, and share them with others in the game. It succeeded in getting individuals to think differently about how to solve problems in the communities. Consider this outcome versus the likely outcome had the World Bank simply decided to create an information-sharing platform. How many young people might have become involved?

Whether or not games can single-handedly change the world, we know that they have a unique power to motivate and engage. In a recent talk McGonigal described their power this way. Here she refers to the photo of a gamer:

> Notice a few nuances here, the crinkle of the eyes up and around the mouth is a sign of optimism. And the eyebrows up, is surprise. This is a gamer on the verge of something called an epic win. . . . An epic win is an outcome that is so extraordinarily positive you had no idea it was even possible until you achieved it. It was almost beyond the threshold of imagination. And when you get there you are shocked to discover what you are truly capable of. That is an epic win. This is a gamer on the verge of an epic win. And this is the face that we need to see on millions of problem-solvers all over the world as we try to tackle the obstacles of the next century. The face of someone who, against all odds, is on the verge of an epic win.[2]

SEVEN THINGS WE KNOW ABOUT LEARNING

This face on the verge of an epic win is the kind of face that educators can only dream about, right? Not necessarily. As I've pointed out, we have learned something from the gaming world about inspiring this kind of engagement, commitment, and motivation. One person who thinks about this a lot is Tom Chatfield, an arts and book editor at the U.K. current-affairs magazine *Prospect* and author of *Fun, Inc.,* in which he offers a defense of the status of computer games in our culture. Chatfield considers himself a game theorist. He is interested in exploring neurological research on how games draw on our pleasure centers and using this information to understand how to improve our world, including how to educate our children. In a 2010 talk, he identified seven ways games reward the brain. To understand how to motivate learning and how games specifically can be used to motivate learning, let's look at these seven ways:

1. *Continuous grading.* Most games give participants the ability to watch their progress slowly but surely creep along in infinitesimal increments. This might look like a bar graph, or a figure in a race, but somehow how the gamer is doing overall is clearly displayed and communicated.

2. *Multiple long- and short-term aims that are clearly defined.* It is always clear in a game what the aims are but this doesn't mean they are simple. They can exist on multiple fronts and reward multiple forms of success.

3. *Rewarding effort.* In most games you get credit every time you do something. Engaging helps you make progress. You are never punished for failure; you are only rewarded for trying and for success.

4. *Feedback.* Feedback is immediate and continuous. This means gamers can fail in millions of small ways, learn quickly what they need to change, and then move on.

5. *Element of uncertainty.* There are enough surprising experiences and rewards, pitched at just the right level of uncertainty so that gamers don't get lulled into boredom or complacency. Experiences that surprise just enough can create high engagement by tapping into a powerful evolutionary mechanism.

6. *Finding windows of learning.* There are moments of engagement, points when learning is taking place at an enhanced level, when it is best to give people something they need to remember. Brain research confirms this and game designers often know how to exploit it.

7. *Confidence.* The result is not just enhanced learning but confidence. Game playing and its reward systems make people braver, more willing to take risks, and harder to discourage.[3]

Most of what Chatfield describes wouldn't come as a surprise to experienced and effective teachers but many of these teachers would probably be the first to admit that trying to calibrate these experiences as carefully as game designers do is almost impossible without help. We can set up reward systems, help students track their progress, and try hard to reward effort and success and not punish failure, but can we do it with anything like the efficiency, persistence, and finely calibrated stages of the best-designed games? As Chatfield says in that same speech, not only does he love video games but he's "also slightly in awe of them." He continues, "I'm in awe of their power in terms of imagination, in terms of technology, in terms of concept. But I think, above all, I'm in awe at their power to motivate, to compel us, to transfix us, like really nothing else we've ever invented has quite done before. And I think that we can learn some pretty amazing things by looking at how we do this."[4]

BRINGING GAMING TO SCHOOL

Educators are beginning to draw on the power of games in schools throughout the country. But we are just scratching the surface. There are still many people who are resistant, thinking the games are too violent, too unlike learning in the real world, or simply not powerful enough to wrap a curriculum around. Games like Oregon Trail, Reader Rabbit, and Where in the World Is Carmen San Diego? were often used as supplemental curriculum but were too limited to help students who were struggling with math or learning to read. That is changing. As Chatfield points out, the new generation of computer games are adaptive—they adjust the level of difficulty to the players, finding students' instructional levels, where they learn best, and offering just enough of a challenge to get them learning. The world of educational computing games is becoming more and more effective in drawing on this technology and has enormous potential for helping students practice and develop basic skills. This can be a particularly effective way to reach students who for various reasons may not come to our schools with the support and motivation necessary to dedicate themselves to more traditional forms of learning. We know that boys, for example, are not competing well with girls, who are now making up the greater percentage of college students.

BEYOND BASIC SKILLS—SIMULATING REALITY

The University of the Pacific Dental School uses simulations to allow dental students to screw up their first root canal in a virtual environment rather than on an unsuspecting patient. The American Association of Colleges of Pharmacy recommends simulations to its 120-member colleges to develop critical thinking skills around therapy management. The Department of Defense operates the most sophisticated human development systems in the world with Lockheed-developed jet fighter and naval battle simulations. The Army trains soldiers for reconnaissance with virtual Afghan villages. Games and simulations can do much more than help children practice basic skills. As Jane McGonigal, the nonprofit game designer we met in the opening of the chapter, suggests, games can help us learn about reality, prepare us to engage with reality, and, in fact, test out alternate realities.

53

"Good gameplay is really science," according to Scot Osterweil, who is quoted in a recent *USA Today* article about a collaborative online educational game that began in April 2011. Osterweil is creative director of MIT's Education Arcade, an organization that is devoted to researching and developing projects on the learning that naturally occurs with games and the design of games. He is further quoted observing that with good games, "[y]ou come into a situation that is chaotic and it doesn't make sense. You observe. You begin to probe and you test. Then you get some feedback. You form a hypothesis and refine your response, and you do more tests and eventually you solve the problem."[5]

PREDICTIONS

In five years . . .

Instant feedback from learning games, simulations, and virtual environments will be widely used, resulting in more persistence and time on task.

Vanished is an environmental mystery game published by Scot Osterweil's team at the Education Arcade at MIT. Offered free during April and May 2011 in conjunction with the Smithsonian Institution, "the game encouraged students to do the real work of science: they hypothesize, investigate, and collaborate."[6]

Kids do real-world experiments and activities, including visiting one of the seventeen participating museums, that mesh with the fiction of the game. "It is both a development and a research project," said Osterweil. "What we want to see is whether, through this type of activity, kids evince real scientific reasoning."[7]

The Education Arcade has created two reports (*Moving Learning Games Forward* and *Using the Technology of Today in the Classroom Today*), both of which are available on their website (www.educationarcade.org/). In *Moving Learning Games Forward,* Education Arcade discusses the role that play has in learning and observes that a child at play is exercising freedom along five distinct axes: freedom to fail, freedom to experiment, freedom to fashion identities, freedom of effort, and freedom of interpretation. Some of these echo the seven rewards identified by Tom Chatfield, such as the freedom to fail and the freedom of effort. But it is interesting to note just how important the other freedoms—to fashion identities and to interpret—figure into learning and in motivating children to learn. As the report explains, games give children the freedom to try on identities and to practice when to be aggressive or cooperative. The report also points to a challenge for those designing learning games that children bring their own interpretations and their own individual, social, and cultural motivations to play. Yes, games can motivate children but not all children will be motivated or will respond in the same way.

The collaborative online learning game mentioned in the article is conducted by the Smithsonian and MIT. Similar to EVOKE it allows children to participate from all over the country in a collaborative community to solve a science-fiction mystery involving a fictitious environmental disaster with real-world scientists from the Smithsonian in areas such as paleobiology, entomology, and forensic anthropology. This kind of real-world simulation not only allows children to test out their problem-solving skills but also allows them the freedom to be scientists alongside real scientists and see what that's like. They are testing not just their ideas but also themselves in an arena beyond their classroom and beyond their homes.

QUEST TO LEARN—A GAME-BASED SCHOOL

Imagine a school based on game theory. Middle schoolers might salivate over the idea and parents might worry that by sending their children to such a school they are essentially waving a white flag and letting the games have their way. Perhaps they are, but what this chapter puts forth is how games can be harnessed for learning. Quest to Learn (Q2L) is a middle school in Manhattan started in 2009 by Katie Salen, a professor of design and technology at Parsons The New School for Design, and Robert Torres, a learning scientist who is a former school principal. Along with a team of game designers, they have created a curriculum with gaming at the center; students not only play games to learn, they also learn to design games. The Quest to Learn website says the school "[p]urposely responded not only to the growing evidence that digital media and games offer powerful models for reconsidering how and where young people learn, but also to the belief that access for all students to these opportunities is critical."[8] Currently, the student body is composed of about 150 sixth- and seventh-graders but the plan is for Quest to Learn to eventually expand through the twelfth grade.

Although it is too early to fully understand how the learning at Quest to Learn compares with that at traditional middle schools, a lengthy article in the *New York Times Magazine* paints a profile of engaged and excited students performing complex tasks.[9] The following Q2L glossary from the Quest to Learn website also provides an excellent window into what goes on in this school.

Q2L Glossary

Being Me: a school-based social network site where students can communicate, post work, collaborate, and reflect.

Being, Space and Place: a class connecting social studies with reading and writing fiction, non-fiction, poetry, and comics.

Boss Level: two-week "intensive" where students apply knowledge and skills to date to propose solutions to complex problems.

Codeworlds: a class where math meets ELA and language rules the day.

Home Base: 10 kids + one very interested adult = student advisories that meet twice a day.

Missions: 10-week units that give students a complex problem they must solve.

Mission Lab: Q2L's game design and curriculum development studio.

Quests: challenge-based lessons that make up Missions.

SEL: socio-emotional learning; an approach to teaching the whole child.

SMALLab: mixed reality environment focused on embodied learning.

Smartool: a "tool to think with" created by students as part of their class work.

Sports for the Mind: a class focused on digital media, game design, and mental acrobatics.

The Way Things Work: a cool science and math class where students learn how to take all kinds of systems apart and put them back together again.

Wellness: a class designed to get students moving and thinking about ways to be healthy, from nutrition, to sports, to mental and emotional health.[10]

CHANGING THE GAME OF LEARNING

Michael Levine, the executive director of the Joan Ganz Cooney Center, an independent research and innovation group devoted to literacy development for diverse learners, notes, "[We] believe that the demonstrated potential of digital media wisely guided by caring adults could become a 'game changer' in advancing children's prospects in the decade ahead."[11] If we are committed to reaching and motivating all students and if we are committed to giving them the skills they need for a digital world, we need to harness the power of learning games and engaging media.

Daphne Bavelier, a professor of brain and cognitive sciences at the University of Rochester, studies young people playing action video games. Having now conducted more than twenty studies on the topic, Bavelier says, "It turns out that action video games are far from mindless." National Public Radio reported that "[h]er studies show that video gamers show improved skills in vision, attention and certain aspects of cognition. And these skills are not just gaming skills, but real-world skills. They perform better than non-gamers on certain tests of attention, speed, accuracy, vision and multitasking, says Bavelier."[12]

SMART LEARNING IN THE MILITARY

In 2008, I asked a professor to bring together the smartest people she knew to talk about breakthroughs in learning. I was frustrated to see military officers on the list and couldn't imagine that they would have much to add to the conversation. I was wrong. Retired vice admiral Al Harms, who led the learning revolution in the Navy, turned out to be the star participant on an education panel. The following year, I had the opportunity to speak at a military training and simulation conference (I/TSEC). It became quite clear that the U.S. military is the most sophisticated, large-scale human development organization in the world. They are remarkably good at defining job competencies, identifying skill gaps, and building training experiences—including game technology—to fit the need. They work with external partners such as Lockheed and Boeing to build elaborate training simulations for training jet pilots and ship crews and to integrate these into a training program that draws on multiple modes of learning. Lockheed and its military customers share incentives to create a rapid path to mastery that involves not just engaging trainees in simulation games—although these play an important role, for instance, troops can train for field reconnaissance by visiting a virtual village full of good guys and bad guys—but also coming up with the optimal mix of online learning, simulation, classroom interaction, and actual flight time. This kind of learning is not just effective, it is cost efficient. Lockheed trains pilots in more than two dozen countries, often with performance contracts that encourage cost savings.

Richard Boyd, who heads up Lockheed's Virtual World Labs, an informal group of engineers and technologists from all of Lockheed's business units working on improving human performance using game technology, describes what cost-effective training for mastery looks like. In a personal interview, Boyd discussed a recent contract between Lockheed and the United Kingdom:

The U.K. ministry of defense has tapped Lockheed Martin to train all of its aircrew for the next 25 years. It is one of the most amazing contracts I have seen in my career. It is set up the way all human endeavors should be, with perfectly aligned incentives. Here is how it works: The U.K. provides us with candidates they deem to be qualified to become jet fighter pilots, helicopter pilots or cargo plane pilots or air crew aboard those aircraft. We are completely responsible for their training. We must determine how much time should be spent in a real aircraft, how much time in a simulator, how much time with interactive multimedia instruction, how much time with classroom instruction and how much time in self-study. Lockheed Martin is only paid when a qualified aircrew member is produced. We have every incentive in the world to determine the shortest path to mastery. The results have been what you might predict. More pilots trained at a lower cost in a shorter amount of time than anyone predicted. Armed with this knowledge of how different kinds of students respond to different training media for different kinds of tasks compels us to see if we can apply this knowledge to improving our lagging education system. What if we could achieve 12th grade competency in the U.S. in only ten grades? Or nine? Perhaps we move students into the work force early, or use the extra time for more mastery; or community service. These are the ideas that motivate me to continue to press these simulation capabilities forward in an accelerating information age.[13]

There are at least four things that K–12 education can learn from the military and specifically the relationship with Lockheed. First, both partners are relentlessly committed to creating rapid pathways to mastery and the flexibility to test ways to blend different components and types of learning for different types of students. They approach human development challenges with an innovation mindset. Second, they simulate stakes that matter. Because the military is training for life-and-death situations, it's key that some of the training be conducted under the stress of realistic simulations but with the safety to fail. K–12 education could use more real-world-connected learning—more opportunities for students to see why learning matters and to experience the consequences of actions. Simulations, internships, and service learning experiences can all help make learning real and can allow students to succeed and fail with a safety net. Third, the military is really good at job preparation. They accurately map job competencies, create effective training pathways, and certify preparation. Some community colleges do this well, but career and technical training is pretty haphazard in the United States compared to the systematic approach taken by the military and the Scandinavian countries. An efficient pathway that connected high school and career training to the likelihood of family wage employment would be a big motivator for some young people. And finally, the military creates learning partnerships with organizations that can share the risk, make investments, and make them smarter.

When pressed to name the most important national security issue, retired vice admiral Harms did not mention terrorism—he points to what will happen in U.S. classrooms over the next ten years. Unless the sector, beginning with the Department of Education, embraces the private sector, creates a substantial and focused R&D agenda, and encourages private investment, U.S. education won't make much improvement and we won't learn all that we could from the world's best military (and learning organization).

It's time for schools to get in the game.

EQUALIZATION

Connecting All Students to Excellence

I won the genetic lottery: I was born in the United States to great parents, had every educational opportunity, received several job offers out of school, and had rich continuing education options. That birth trajectory resulted in a level of personal access to language, experience, people, capital, and technology unusual among the other seven billion people on the planet.

Louis Gomez of the Carnegie Foundation for the Advancement of Teaching talks about the two Americas: in "Growth America" young people have access to good schools, good teachers, and extended learning options including lots of books, museum visits, and trips abroad. In "Decline America" the schools are stagnant, learning opportunities are limited, and young people's experiences are restricted if not depraved.

The premise of this book is that learning technology can help young people learn more faster, but it can also do something that has been stumping educators since education began: it can narrow the learning opportunity gap. Learning technology, with cheap access devices and broadband, can extend access to learning content, tools, and professionals. Low-income students have always faced two disadvantages: weak schools and less opportunity to learn outside of school. Personal digital learning is extending access to the same courses and the same effective educators to all students regardless of their neighborhood school and it's available 24/7. Learning technology will help close the preparation gap—more students will leave high school eligible for college and ready to earn credit without remediation. (You'll note that I didn't predict that personal digital learning will narrow the achievement gap; I'm less certain about that. It certainly raises the floor—more kids will get a good education—but it also blows away the ceiling. Personal digital learning will be of as much benefit to the gifted student as the struggling student but in the process it will connect millions of young people to viable economic opportunities that they have no access to today.)

TED

The Internet has brought access to everyone. We all have access to the experts, the innovators, and the products of their labors. We have access to each other and to almost anyone who can teach us something. We can define new communities, teach ourselves, teach others. No one needs to be left out. This recently created ability for anyone to learn anything is so world changing that it defies description in a paragraph or a chapter.

TED CONFERENCE

Over four days, fifty speakers each take an eighteen-minute slot, and there are many shorter presentations, including music, performance, and comedy. There are no breakout groups. Everyone shares the same experience. It shouldn't work, but it does. It works because all of knowledge is connected. Every so often it makes sense to emerge from the trenches we dig for a living and ascend to a thirty-thousand-foot view, where we see, to our astonishment, an intricately interconnected whole.[1]

But let me illustrate the point by zeroing in on a single point of access: the TED talks now available on www.TED.com.

You may have noticed in previous chapters that many of the thinkers and innovators I've cited have been on TED. It wasn't necessarily through this website that I was introduced to these people but it is through TED that everyone can hear their most exciting ideas. TED, a nonprofit organization that's been around since 1987, is devoted to "ideas worth spreading" and stands for technology, entertainment, and design. The TED Conference held annually in Long Beach features an eclectic array of speakers on science, business, the arts, and global issues. The event sells out a year in advance so now I just watch TED videos at my convenience. It was in a recent TED talk that I came upon one of the clearest descriptions of how computers are changing access to education.

A BRIEF HISTORY OF ACCESS

In this recent talk social studies teacher Diane Laufenberg tells the history of access. She showed a slide of her grandmother's graduation picture from eighth grade, two rows of students, five girls and seven boys, who were lucky enough to have access to a school. She explained something that is obvious but powerful. Her grandmother went to the schoolhouse because that's where the information lived. It was in the books that were in the schoolhouse and it was in the teacher's head and that's where you had to go to get it. Laufenberg then fast-forwarded to her own educational experience, which was influenced by having something remarkable in her home: a set of encyclopedias. "It was extraordinary," says Laufenberg, "because I did not have to wait to go to the library to get the information; the information was inside my house and it was awesome." She then moved forward to her own experience as a teacher at the Science Leadership Academy in Philadelphia where there is a one-to-one laptop program and the kids are "bringing laptops with them everyday, taking them home, getting access to information." She then poses the big question: "Why do you have kids come to school if they no longer have to come there to get the information?"[2]

This is an important question and her answer is interesting and significant. She explains how our new closeness to information forces schools to think of themselves not simply as places to get information but as places where children will be challenged and guided in new ways to use information. As more skill-building and content-sharing activities are offered automatically, schools and teachers can increasingly focus on the important stuff: critical thinking (what does this mean?), coherence (where does this fit?), and application (what could I do with this knowledge?). Many of the schools and programs profiled in this book reveal educators doing just that. The other significant implication of Laufenberg's story is that technology is the great equalizer—it can extend access to high-quality learning experiences to almost everyone.

THE GREAT EQUALIZER

It's clear that great teachers, more than any other factor, boost student learning. Unfortunately there just aren't enough great teachers around. *Opportunity at the Top*, a Public Impact report, demonstrates that, under the best possible scenario, all the current reform efforts combined won't put a good teacher in every classroom.[3] How can we stretch the impact of our best teachers over many more students? An online curriculum allows great teachers to have an impact in places where they can't necessarily always show up to—rural areas, the inner cities—and it can extend the influence of teachers in hard-to-staff subject areas such as math and science. Online learning is the only possible way to offer a comprehensive, well-taught, rigorous, college-prep curriculum everywhere. Connecting special needs students and teachers with specialists through videoconferencing will become commonplace.

As we will see in some of the profiles of online education in Chapter Six, an engaging online curriculum that allows students to progress at their own pace can free the classroom teacher from being the primary transmitter of content, giving teachers more time to guide, extend, apply, and intervene with students. And it gives the great teachers more time to mentor junior teachers and staff members. The result is that more students are receiving the benefits of great teachers. The technology effectively provides the impetus for schools to rethink how the teaching profession is structured. This means moving beyond the old one-teacher, one-class model to one in which students spend some of their day with tutors or entry-level teachers who are trained and whose work is overseen by the best teachers.

KHAN ACADEMY

Salman Khan is the new but unlikely face of the learning revolution. He's not a credentialed teacher but with an MBA from Harvard and three degrees from MIT, Sal knows math. After tutoring his cousins online in 2004, schedules got complicated so Sal started making tutorial videos and posting them on YouTube. Sal's easy-to-understand approach and low-key style went viral. In 2006, Sal quit his day job at an investment fund and launched Khan Academy, a nonprofit organization. By March 2011, there were more than 2,200 tutorial videos on his site, he had attracted lots of grant funding, and his site was visited by more than half a million students monthly.

Sal's videos are part of the just-in-time, bite-size, and customized learning future. Did he set out to improve math education? No. Did he set out to start a business? No. The reason Khan Academy evolved and now has the reach that it does is because of one simple and powerful thing: the way he teaches works. He is a great teacher who has extended his reach across the world by simply posting his lessons on YouTube.

Many students are sitting in math classes all over the country confused and bored, then they go home and listen to a few of Khan's brief lessons and they understand. Khan Academy is being adopted by schools as part of their math curriculum. It's also being incorporated into several next-generation learning platforms that offer multiple ways to learn a concept (i.e., lectures, games, and tutorials). It's an example of the free or low-cost learning applications and tools that are being adopted virally by students and teachers—a broad-based, bottom-up revolution.

CHEAPER AND BETTER THAN TEXTBOOKS

There is enough good digital curriculum that it doesn't make sense to buy (or ask students to buy) textbooks anymore. Digital content can be more engaging, it's easier to update, it's more portable, and it is cheaper—in fact, some of it is free. Although in the past free education resources—often referred to as open education resources (OER)—have not had the consistent quality, vetting, or organized connection to standards that schools want and need, that is now changing.

OER Commons and Curriki are efforts to organize open content on one big public library. CK-12 and Flat World Knowledge are creating free textbooks. Other platforms are organizing open content into units of study around the new Common Core State Standards. These efforts are bringing such an adequate level of oversight, organization, and accessibility to open digital curriculum that many schools have felt comfortable turning to these online resources as a way to cut costs.

It is time for states and districts to plan for the shift from print to digital. Most states are broke, some are cutting days out of the school calendar. Districts are laying off teachers and trying to maintain the old way of doing things. But instead of using computers as a cost-effective way to provide access to learning we are creating what seems to be a costly parallel system in which there are lots of computers (about one computer for every 3.5 students) and lots of textbooks but not quite enough of either. If we swapped most of the computers and most of the textbooks for low-cost tablet computers with digital content, schools could extend and improve learning.

K–12 schools in the United States spend about 5 percent of their budgets on instructional materials, tutoring, testing, and instructional technology.[4] If the total per-student spending is about $10,000, schools could redeploy at least some of the $500 per student over the next few years. As content and devices become less expensive, schools will be able to purchase more digital learning services targeting specific needs. The roughly $8 billion spent annually on textbooks amounts to about $150 for every student, the price of a tablet computer running Google's Android operating system. Buying textbooks and asking kids to cart them around is swiftly becoming an expensive relic.

As content and computers get cheaper, we'll see schools clear their server closets and adopt cloud-based services for content management, assessment, data tracking, reporting, as well as specialized instruction and 24/7 tutoring. The one tech support guy with responsibility for five thousand desktops won't have to walk around and update each computer, it will all be done remotely and automatically. Some categories of premium content will flourish—if OER becomes the "basic cable" of education, there will be premium channels for games, simulations, STEM (science and technology) content, special education, English as a second language, and dual-enrollment courses.

Powerful learning software will only get cheaper as software development platforms such as Ruby on Rails continue to

---

PREDICTIONS

In five years . . .

All U.S. students will have access to online courses for Advanced Placement, high-level STEM (science and technology) courses, and any foreign language.

dramatically reduce the cost and time to develop new applications. Ruby is open software—free for anyone to use and modify—and supported by lots of free ways to learn how to use it: videos, chat groups, and searchable libraries. It used to be that we tried to find ways in our budgets to buy computers and other technologies that we viewed as enhancements. Now, inexpensive hardware and software are delivering engaging content and becoming the backbone of the academic system.

A CULTURE OF LEARNING

One of the reasons parents want to send their children to elite schools is not just so they can have access to great teachers and a great curriculum. They also want their children to meet and work with other students who are interested and motivated. Although administrators may be loathe to admit it, most large high schools have a student-driven culture. In good schools, leaders create an intentional culture and coherent structure around productive aims and norms. This is important now but it will become even more important as personal digital learning allows for more choice and customization and carries education away from the school and into the home and elsewhere. Social networks have enhanced a web of relationships for most people connected to the Internet. They can help build a common culture and help make sense of a confusing world—and increasingly do so for school communities. In this new web sociology that provides community access, networks become more important than neighborhoods. Facebook changed how we interact. By the end of this decade, it is likely that social learning groups, not classrooms, will be how learning is organized for many students. Social networks will augment and then replace the classroom as the dominant organizing unit of learning. Although many students will matriculate at their own rate, they will do most of their learning as part of a virtual community.

How is this happening now in schools? Edmodo is a great example of a free and effective social learning platform that is widely adopted. For the cost of a couple servers, two Chicago-area school district tech directors built Edmodo on weekends and evenings over a couple months. With an investment of $1.5 million it became the largest and fastest-growing social learning platform. It was released in Chicago in 2009 and by the end of the year, nearly a third of its three hundred thousand users were international; it doubled in size by the beginning of school in September 2010 and hit one million users by Thanksgiving.

Edmodo allows teachers and students to connect in powerful ways. For teachers who grew up on social networks, Edmodo is very intuitive. Teachers can create ad hoc communities and project teams with their students, communicate with them on their computers and smart phones, link students to relevant material on the Internet, respond to student questions, hold discussions, and even connect to networks of students across the country who might be studying the same thing. At the most basic level, this kind of software takes the teacher out of the school environment and puts her in the student's home and even in front of the student while he is out and about during the day with his smart phone. But this also puts students in contact with one another. A motivated student might send a message to all if he sees something that relates to, say, something they have just discussed either online or in class. Shy students can make their case.

Other social platforms connect students with shared interests—low-income schools to affluent schools, U.S. schools to African schools. Rather than forming communities (or gangs) based solely on what block you grew up on or whether you're on the football team, students, guided by teachers who are interested in creating an intentional culture of learning, can connect to students who might also be interested in art, rap, or photography. It is increasingly possible for students studying the same thing at the same time to connect—more than one hundred thousand students are taking AP History right now. Some of their reasons for connecting will not be as noble as we'd like, so we'll need to stay on top of this, but there is a big, underexploited peer-to-peer learning opportunity.

ADVICE AND SUPPORT

Schools serve a lot of functions, and access to a great education often means access to a whole set of services, mentors, and helpful adults who pave the way to college, career, and making good choices. Here are two examples of how entrepreneurs in education technology have helped provide access to two important services.

Michael Carter noticed in high school and then during his first year of college how lucky he had been to be raised in a household committed to his education and supportive of his college-selection process. With a little investigation, Michael learned that it was a haphazard process for most young people and that, in many cases, students did not make the best possible choice for college. "The college application process, like navigating the job search process for the first time, is not rocket science. However, both are often confusing, counterintuitive and very time-consuming. Most important, both are subjective—there is no such thing as the best college, despite what the *US News and World Report* would like you to believe."[5]

During his freshman year at Washington University, Michael formed Strive for College Collaborative, a nonprofit organization dedicated to helping low-income students prepare for and make the best possible postsecondary selection. Michael's persistent recruiting resulted in a star-studded board of IT entrepreneurs and his fundraising created a great employment opportunity after graduation. Strive is creating chapters on college campuses around the country and building an online decision-support platform for students and families. "Strive is building a movement of undergraduates to mentor low-income students one-on-one through the process of selecting and applying to college. As college students have recently completed the process successfully and are within a few years of age of the students with whom they are working, they are uniquely qualified to provide both the critical information and motivation that many low-income students lack. Strive combines the mentoring with a technology system that helps students identify the colleges that are a best-fit for them given their personal preferences and academic profile."[6] Recently, Nobel laureate economist Joseph Stiglitz delivered a speech to a Strive for College audience in which he articulated the stakes involved: "Our economy would be achieving hundreds of billions of dollars more if those with lower incomes had the same access to education as those of the rest of our society."[7]

Online guidance systems will soon be the backbone of secondary education. They will promote study skills and personal management and they will improve course selection and build career and college awareness. Online guidance systems will support counselors and advisors in helping students navigate the college application process and make this all-important postsecondary decision.

After attending Stanford Graduate School of Business, Jack Lynch and Clay Whitehead looked for a place where technology could make a difference in education. They narrowed their search to speech therapy, found the best people in the country to advise them, and launched Presence TeleCare. Their high-quality, interactive, online speech therapy solves two problems; for many schools, it is difficult to retain full-time speech therapists, and many therapists want to work part-time from home. Presence TeleCare creates an elegant technology solution to an educational problem and a flexible labor market for at-home workers. Clay summed up the problem they attack: "Speech pathologists help kids with a variety of conditions and a very large number of kids eligible for care are not getting that care because of a huge shortage of those teachers. A Department of Education report suggests that 60% of schools are short and can't meet their IEP mandates. There are a lot of kids not getting the help they need."[8] Schools save money and gain scheduling flexibility. Therapists can work as many hours as they want, when they want, where they want. Clay continued:

> Jack and I were inspired to start this company, in large part, because of our personal experiences with communication disabilities. I had learning disabilities and did not learn how to read until very late, while Jack has a family member with Autism. We realized that there is a massive need out there for special education services that we could address by using the web to bring together teachers from all over the country. It proved out almost immediately. The first client we had went from stuttering 36% of the time to 2% of the time in just a few months, and we got similarly strong results with our first school district. We've grown quickly and are now in 8 states.[9]

As these stories and the examples outlined in this chapter show, for the first time in our nation's history there is an opportunity to provide every student with access to quality learning experiences, which means the technology is scalable— it can expand and be used on large and small scales. For students trapped in struggling schools, personalized digital learning, online communities, and great teachers online have the potential to create a positive learning culture and sequences of successful learning experiences. We need to stop thinking of technology as something we add on to the current "batch-print" system (batch processing students by age through flat and sequential print curriculum); instead, we need to view personal digital learning as the new backbone of a smart learning system that will help more students leave prepared for college and careers.

A WORLD OF LEARNING

Beyond or outside the K–12 world there is an explosion of learning resources. In addition to tools such as Wikipedia and search, peer-to-peer learning sites pop up every week. WiZiQ is a website that offers software for connecting teachers and students online and has about seventy thousand registered teachers who hold regular classes, some for free and some for a fee. P2PU allows anyone to offer courses online. When formal certifications don't exist or work very well, for example for web developers, P2PU wants to use portfolios and references to create new

PREDICTIONS

In five years . . .

Half of states and districts will stop buying print textbooks and will shift to customizable digital texts and open education resources.

ways to demonstrate competence and support a free (or nearly free) approach to job preparation.

It's getting easier to find free college courses online or at least free lectures from the world's leading scholars on sites such as iTunes U and Academic Earth. With all of this free learning, few colleges can justify charging $30,000 or more in tuition. High schools can't maintain the old master schedule with limited and traditional offerings with so much access to quality courses and effective teachers. Elementary schools can't explain away why some students reach the fourth grade and can't read.

It changes everything when anyone can learn anything almost anywhere.

INTEGRATION

Putting It All Together to Make Schools Smarter

Customization, motivation, equalization—these are good things. You may even be convinced that personal digital learning has the potential to transform U.S. education and then extend access to quality learning to the next billion young people in emerging and developing economies. But you also may wonder what happens when you try to activate this potential in the complex and resilient world of schools. Will technology remain an expensive add-on? Will budget cutting stall progress instead of accelerating it? Will the next round of state tests lock in the old model for another decade? Will the short-term interests of local school boards, teachers unions, administrators, and colleges continue to block innovation? In Chapter Seven, I address how policies must change in order to make a friendly environment for digital learning and innovation, but in this chapter I describe models of real schools that are really and truly mobilizing the potential of personal digital learning to make a difference in students' lives, offering them customized learning, motivating them with innovative curricula, and providing access to excellence for thousands of students.

LEARNING ONLINE

More than four million U.S. K–12 students were enrolled in formal online learning programs in 2011. We can probably double that number if we include students who made extensive use of skill-building software in a classroom or used online curriculum in a school lab to make up a lost credit. About 3.5 million students learned predominantly at home; a tenth of the home-educated students were enrolled in virtual public charter schools.

All together, more than 12 percent of U.S. students did a significant portion of their learning online, with a higher percentage in high school—and a much higher percentage if we included all the online learning that happens outside of school. Online learning will continue to grow at more than 40 percent annually, doubling every three years. About half of U.S. school districts are operating or planning online learning programs.[1] In 2008, the authors of *Disrupting Class* predicted that by 2020, the majority of high school students in the United States will do the majority of their learning online, and it's now clear that it will be sooner than that.[2]

Schools that offer a large part of the curriculum online are often referred to as *blended* (or *hybrid*) schools. For the next generation, most online learning will be done at a school where students will experience a blend of online and on-site learning. Many students will blend their own learning—choosing an online course over a traditional course for acceleration, remediation, or scheduling purposes—but increasingly, online learning will be intentionally incorporated into school models.

I define blended learning as a shift in instructional responsibility to an online or computer-mediated environment for at least part of a student's day with the inten-

PREDICTIONS

In five years . . .

Innovative mobile learning models used in India will be adopted by several U.S. districts.

tion of improving both learning and operating productivity. In other words, doing things differently for better results. For a long time, the education sector never worried about, never even thought about, productivity. But that is starting to change, beginning with the effects of the recent recession, which encouraged a few people to think about doing better for less. The Department of Education mentioned productivity in the 2010 National Education Technology Plan—the first time it has suggested that technology will be an integral part of doing better with less in what Secretary Duncan called the "new normal" in this postrecession period.[3]

For education reformers and foundations, charter schools have been a hoped-for proving ground of productivity. Foundations have probably invested $1 billion in an effort to build and expand high-quality charter school management organizations (CMOs).

None of the CMOs have proved to be as scalable or sustainable as initially predicted—that's partially because charters get less money than traditional schools and typically don't get public facilities. CMOs were supposed to be self-sustaining after opening one or two dozen schools—that's typically not the case (especially in California where costs are high and reimbursement rates are low). Budget cuts after the Great Recession have made it even harder to sustain a charter school without donations. Some of the national donors, frustrated by the lack of scalability and sustainability, have been pushing charter school networks to think about new school models that are less expensive to operate during the next decade. These schools are turning to online learning and creating blended models as an approach to increasing productivity.

THE BLENDED MENU

As the following models will show, blended school formats can help schools achieve cost efficiencies by significantly extending learning time, allowing students to spend more time each day and more days each year in productive learning activities without costing any more money. Customized learning also allows many students to finish high school faster—skipping the typically wasted senior year—saving the state and the family money.

Here are profiles of a number of schools along the blended learning continuum.

1. *School of One.* A math program in the New York City public schools that draws on multiple modes of instruction. This innovative double-block period is currently a *partial blend* (because the rest of the day is traditional) but it provides a compelling picture of customized learning.

Schools on the Blended Learning Continuum

2. *Rocketship Education.* A network of elementary charter schools using a *partial blended* model in which students attend a traditional school but spend about one-fourth of the day in a digital learning lab.

3. *Kunskapsskolan.* A highly individualized Swedish model in which most of the learning is mediated online but where students attend physical schools that look more like an Internet café than a classroom.

4. *AdvancePath Academics.* A *blended* network of drop-out prevention academies for overaged and undercredited youth. Students attend a physical school but engage in a fully online education with on-site support and guidance.

5. *K12.* A national network of online schools including a virtual charter school in Virginia operated by K12. Online teachers and at-home learning coaches support student learning.

SCHOOL OF ONE

When Joel Rose was chief human resource officer of the New York City schools, he began imagining a new way to teach math. His goal was to customize math instruction so that students would be spending time only on what they needed to learn and would be learning in a way that worked best for them.

He described the idea to Chancellor Klein who encouraged him to run a summer school pilot in 2009. During the second half of the 2009–10 school year, School of One became the core math instructional program for sixth grade at a New York middle school. The following year, School of One became the middle-grade math program at three New York middle schools.

Instead of reporting to a math class with a single teacher, students report to School of One, a double classroom that has a variety of learning stations equipped with laptops for each student and with teachers who engage with students in different ways depending on the student's tailor-made program. You might see eighty students, some at tables in front of laptops working independently or with online tutors, others in small groups, some conferencing one-on-one with teachers, and some playing online learning games. How does this work?

At the heart of School of One is a computer program developed by Brooklyn-based Wireless Generation. Rose worked closely with the company to come up with the algorithm that customizes math instruction every day for every student. Considering a range of factors—a student's academic history and profile, assessment data from the previous day's work, student interests, best learning modality, available content, staffing, and space—the algorithm generates a recommended plan for the day that is evaluated by teachers, adjusted if necessary, and then flashed on a big screen that looks a lot like an airport terminal departure board. At the end of the day, students take a short assessment that helps to generate another recommended playlist for the following day.

The result, as a 2010 article in the *Atlantic* describes, is that "one student might learn to add fractions at a dry-erase board with a small group, while another uses the Internet to practice calculating the area of a circle with a tutor in Kentucky, while still another student learns about factoring through a game on his laptop."[4]

The term *playlist* is used deliberately; the term and the picture it conjures is, in and of itself, an important contribution to the sector. Those of us that have seen and read about School of One now have a vivid picture of customized learning—a playlist for learning like the playlist of music that iTunes Genius helps create for our iPods. You'll now find playlists on a number of sites including MyHomeLearning.com from the New York City–based nonprofit Computers for Youth sites.

The more data School of One collects, the more effective it becomes at generating playlists, making it a powerful tool for educators and for students. Here are two examples of the benefits of informed instruction. First, the small-group instruction at School of One is unique; every student is ready for that lesson delivered in that fashion—what a gift for teachers! The algorithm determined the most appropriate next lesson and best learning mode. Instead of teaching to the middle of a big class, a School of One teacher has a small group ready to learn. A Freakonomics radio profile illustrated a second benefit of a smart recommendation engine. The reporter zeroed in on a student struggling with algebraic concepts. The assessment data reveals that he didn't have the same struggle with geometry. Many teachers seeing this pattern might assume that some students do better with geometry than with algebra. But the algorithm revealed something more nuanced. It showed that the kinds of lessons—the approach to learning— that the student had engaged in for geometry were slightly different from those used to teach him algebra. The recommendation, then, wasn't simply to give him more practice in algebra but to try an approach similar to the way he had learned geometry.[5]

This algorithm could not have been created if Rose and his team had not been committed to exploring different modes of learning and ensuring that lessons were clearly categorized according to these modes. For the summer pilot, the School of One team tagged 1,200 lessons of different levels and modes (they now have several times that many). The simplifying assumptions were big forty-minute chunks of learning (which rules out a lot of short-form videos and games) and an independent assessment framework (separate from instruction).

School of One offers only a math program at this point. It doesn't fully capture the benefit of content-embedded assessment (like game scores can). And, although in pilot phase, they haven't attempted to stretch staffing levels to save schools money. Despite these limitations, it still warrants the *Time Magazine* designation as one of the top innovations of 2009. The long-term hope is that the model will prove successful enough to be applied to other subjects.

In October 2010, the New York City Department of Education's Research and Policy Support Group published the findings of their evaluation of School of One in which they compared outcomes on math assessments of School of One participants and those of other students who didn't participate in the program. The findings are detailed in the report titled, "School of One Evaluation—2010 Spring Afterschool and Short-Term In-School Pilot Programs."[6] Here are some of the key findings:

- Students who participated in School of One showed significantly larger gains in math than their peers.

- Participating students had favorable attitudes toward School of One, particularly when earning points on teams, learning from an online teacher, and working with other students.

- School of One teachers showed generally favorable attitudes toward the program. Teachers felt the program helped them learn new approaches to teaching math.

Program development costs have been about $3.3 million with about 70 percent coming from the Robin Hood Foundation and the Michael & Susan Dell Foundation. As they refine the staffing model, the program should become more affordable and eventually may prove to be a better and cheaper way to deliver middle-grade math.

ROCKETSHIP EDUCATION

Rocketship Education is a nonprofit elementary charter network that currently operates three elementary campuses serving over 1,200 students in the San Jose, California, area. And they have plans to open hundreds of schools. Founded in 2006, their mission is to "eliminate the achievement gap" in high-poverty neighborhoods.[7] This is a tall order but if they have a chance at making this happen it is because of the blended model they are implementing that they refer to as "a hybrid education model," which has students spending about a quarter of their day in a computer lab and the rest in a traditional classroom.

In education we talk so much about resources. "If only we did that more, we could achieve more." Or, "We need to get rid of bureaucratic waste so we can spend on learning." John Danner, the CEO of Rocketship Education, credits the effective use of online learning with freeing up resources to help students learn and to give them a good environment in which to learn. According to Danner, because the Learning Lab does not require credentialed teachers, Rocketship saves about 25 percent of their salary costs, which comes to about $500,000 a year to reinvest. In a May 2010 advisory meeting, Danner explained that they use this money to give principals a year of training, pay teachers 20 percent more than surrounding districts pay, and support network growth.[8]

But more than this, Rocketship does two very important things: it puts an academic dean at each school who supports and works closely with teachers and it runs a two-hour response-to-intervention after-school program for the bottom 20 percent of students. We know that effective teaching is one of the most, if not the single most, important factors in student learning and by incorporating an academic dean in each school, Rocketship is dedicating itself to good teaching. Also, by letting computers do what they do best—help students work on basic skills—they are freeing teachers up to do what they do best: teach students how to think, get engaged, work cooperatively, and solve problems. Danner is hoping that they can push the hybrid to a 50/50 balance and so eventually double teacher pay to well over $100,000 per year.

The test scores that Rocketship Mateo Sheedy Elementary School in San Jose, California, for example, has achieved are impressive. In 2009 its annual state achievement test scores resulted in a 926 academic performance index score, which was an increase of 35 points over the previous year. To put these scores in context, it was the highest-performing low-income elementary school in San Jose and Santa Clara County and third highest in the whole state of California. How did they achieve this? According to Preston Smith, Rocketship's cofounder and chief achievement officer, it wasn't because they took only the highest performing students, which is a frequent claim by critics of charter schools. (Nearly 73 percent of students at Mateo Sheedy are English language learners and 78 percent qualify for the free and reduced lunch program.) It is by dedicating themselves to identifying and moving lower-achieving students out of the bottom two performance categories: far below basic and below basic. In a press release from Rocketship, Smith explains their thinking about students who need extra support: "Students in these bottom two quintiles have significant problems in whole-class settings because their basic reading, writing, and math issues keep them from understanding. By focusing on moving students out of these bottom two quintiles in their first year at Rocketship, we give them a chance to make their classroom time valuable again."[9]

Danner's team is pushing hard. They already have some of the best academic elementary schools in California, but Rocketship continues to look for more productive learning software and when they find it, they will increase time in the lab. They are building links from the learning lab to the classroom. They are driving down the cost of buildings and building scalable systems. This isn't rocket science but it takes a blended school model and a laser focus on student achievement and opening more schools to serve more students.

KUNSKAPSSKOLAN

Founded in 1999, Kunskapsskolan operates thirty-two secondary schools in Sweden with the mission of providing a personalized education, putting students at the center. Students each have a teacher who acts as a personal tutor and advisor, following them through their high school years, training them in understanding their own learning strategies, following up on their school work, and making herself available in various ways to support students on their own paths through secondary school. The idea is to help students slowly learn how to take more responsibility for their own learning and setting and reaching their own goals so that by the end of their high school careers they are fully independent.

The curriculum is divided into subjects that are mastered either through steps, such as modern languages or math, or through courses, in which several subjects are connected by a theme. Which step a student starts on depends on an initial assessment. For each step there are clear goals that students can move through at their own pace following the plan worked out with their personal teacher-advisor. Each week students meet with their advisor and develop goals for the week, as well as a plan for what kind of lesson formats they will engage in to achieve them. They can choose from lectures, workshops, laboratory experiments, as well many independent online learning lessons. One of the primary organization features of the school is a web portal that outlines the steps for subjects and the tasks involved in each step, describes courses and provides resources, and houses student documents. This is age-appropriate customized education, offering students choices and asking them to take responsibility for their own learning.

Kunskapsskolan schools do not look like a traditional school with rows of classrooms off a long hallway. They are designed to support the varied learning needs and approaches of the individual students and so provide a diversity of work and study spaces. There are small rooms in which students can meet to collaborate on projects, an editorial office where teachers and students can work together, a café that serves as a natural meeting place for teachers and students as well as a place for students to engage in individual online learning, and a lecture hall for presentations, lectures, or other gatherings. A blended curriculum like that at Kunskapsskolan, which relies on a significant online component and enables individual progress, changes the student-teacher relationship as well as how students interact, and the physical format eliminates the basic assumptions around one teacher in a classroom with twenty-five students.

What information we have on outcomes is based on the Swedish national grading system. In 2010, for example, the share of Kunskapsskolan students who achieved the highest grades in the national grading system was 72 percent in English, 45 percent in math, and 68 percent in Swedish—all of which are higher than the national average. But perhaps more telling is that its influence is being felt worldwide. Kunskapsskolan opened a charter school in New York City in September 2011.

ADVANCEPATH ACADEMICS

AdvancePath Academics runs drop-out prevention academies for at-risk students and for those who have already passed their graduation dates without enough credits to receive a diploma. There are about two dozen academies across four different states: California, Alaska, Maryland, and Michigan. Most of the students are seventeen and eighteen years of age but the curriculum ranges from ninth through twelfth grade. AdvancePath is a fully blended school with a curriculum that is fully online and an Internet café–style double classroom where the students receive help, support, tutoring, and small-group work with credentialed teachers.

How is education customized to serve students for whom nothing has worked so far? Many of these students, who have fallen behind academically, are perpetually truant and exhibit behavior problems or have been referred by juvenile justice and have tried a range of programs and approaches to get through high school. Many have enrolled in independent study but found they didn't have the discipline, self-management capacity, or academic skills to follow through. These students, many of whom are adults with adult responsibilities and challenges—jobs, children, sick parents, no place to live—needed a program that was flexible but that had enough oversight and engagement from supportive adults to help them complete it.

AdvancePath offers two to three four-hour learning sessions a day, five days a week, typically attended by forty to fifty students. Students may attend morning, afternoon, or evening (if available) sessions, giving them the flexibility to take care of personal needs. They spend about three-quarters of their time working on online coursework with the support of a team of teachers who are available to check in and help. The balance of the time is teacher-led, small-group instruction, typically involving anywhere from four to eight students. They also spend some time engaging in one-on-one conferences with their caseload teacher. The academies work to help students achieve their unique goals, providing both career and college-planning guidance.

Data collected by AdvancePath for the 2009–10 school year show that approximately nine out of ten enrolled students achieve success, with success defined as graduation, transfer back to the high school to graduate, transfer to another district program, or a verified move to another school district.[10] Another way to look at outcomes is to consider the rate that students accumulate high school credits. Overall, AdvancePath students were achieving approximately 29 percent of the annual credit requirements at the time of their enrollment into the academy. Post–academy enrollment, these students began earning credits an average of 3.5 times faster (or a little faster than the typical student). The online curriculum and a no-nonsense student-driven culture are what allow AdvancePath to help students make this kind progress. By freeing the teachers to work closely with individual students and by allowing the coursework to be tailored to students' academic needs, the online component is the key to AdvancePath's success.

K¹² AND THE VIRTUAL ACADEMIES

Founded by former education secretary Bill Bennet and current CEO Ron Packard, K^{12} is a $500 million publicly traded company worth $1 billion. K^{12} provides online curriculum and instruction from kindergarten through high school. Although it can be purchased and used independently by homeschooling parents, most students engage in this curriculum through the virtual charter schools that are currently operating in thirty states and the District of Colombia. These virtual academies, as they are known, hire credentialed teachers who work directly with students and parents to oversee the students' progress, evaluate work, provide support, and engage students individually and in groups. Students also must have an engaged parent or other adult at home, a learning coach, who oversees their daily activity.

Learning coaches (usually a parent) in grades K–8 work in cooperation with the students' teachers to facilitate progress through the daily lessons and modify the pace and schedule to their child's needs. At the beginning of the year the coach receives a one-hundred-pound shipment of books, worksheets, training videos, science materials, and more. Students in the early grades don't spend more than 20 percent of their time on the computer, so there is a good deal of orchestration and support required from the learning coach. In high school the role of the coach shifts, becoming less involved in direct management of the student's time and progress and more involved in helping the student self-manage.

In the K–8 grades, students are assigned a specific teacher who works directly with the student and the learning coach. These teachers monitor progress, work on helping students to master subject areas and skills, and develop specific interventions as needed when students appear to be struggling. High school courses are taught by different teachers, just as in a traditional high school. Teachers interact directly with students through e-mail and phone, responding to questions, giving feedback on assignments, conducting tutorial sessions, and facilitating whole-class online discussions.

What the virtual academics and K^{12} provide is a well-defined curriculum, some might even call it rigid, with each online lesson being carefully scripted, which can be implemented in the most flexible of ways. This flexibility can make the difference between success and failure for many students. Of course, it isn't for everyone. Many students thrive on showing up at school every day. Many parents need and value the custodial role that schools play or cannot play the role of learning coach. And many teachers prefer to work in an environment in which they interact face-to-face with students and where they see their colleagues, if only in passing, every day. But there are increasing numbers of students and teachers who not only thrive on the flexibility but also appreciate how the program allows them to work one-on-one.

Teaching online from a remote location (such as a home office) has been a widespread option only for the last decade. Becoming an online elementary teacher for Virginia Virtual Academy had a steep learning curve, even for Joyce Voelker, a former principal and veteran teacher: "It took an entirely different skill set." She was skeptical of an online elementary school, but after one year of teaching online has become a wholehearted advocate by seeing the benefit to a wide span of families. "For every student, there is a different reason— behavior issues, health conditions, or students who are just a little different—but they come alive in this program and it is a godsend for these families."[11]

State achievement scores for virtual academies in Ohio and Florida, for example, reveal that their students meet or significantly exceed the state averages in math and reading. But this is a small part of the picture. It is clear that the K[12] curriculum and online approaches can meet and exceed conventional classroom teaching at least insofar as test scores are concerned. But what about the social skills? Many critics of virtual learning point to a lack of social interaction as a potential downside of this approach. But a 2008 study, conducted by Interactive Systems Design in collaboration with The Center for Research in Educational Policy at the University of Memphis, concluded that, according to Dr. Jay Sivin-Kachala, who led the research, "typical, mainstream students enrolled in full-time, online public schools are at least as well-socialized as equivalent students enrolled in traditional public schools."[12] It is important to emphasize that engaging in online learning does not preclude participating in other activities and indeed, because the learning is more efficient, it can allow children more time to interact with other children in environments other than the classroom, where they are likely to experience more success and less stress.

K[12] has been acquiring competitors and curriculum providers to maintain its rapid growth curve. They have developed a blended school model called Flex, piloted in San Francisco, and are selling their digital curriculum to schools to help them develop blended models.

AROUND THE CORNER

By 2014 there will be a wide variety of high-performing blended learning school models that have these five factors in common:

1. Students have 24/7 access to instructional technology.

2. Social networking capabilities are central to instruction and the life of the school.

3. Students benefit from frequent (often instant) academic feedback and learning experiences will be guided by a rich data profile.

4. Students progress based on demonstrated competency.

5. School staffing leverages the knowledge and skill of master teachers supplemented by junior staff and remote teachers and tutors (a differentiated and distributed staffing model).

Blended models will vary on other dimensions including the proportion of the day spent online, how much time students spend at school, and the number of providers involved. In the name of tradition, most blended schools will hang on to the traditional school calendar far beyond usefulness.

As choice to the course—and even lesson—level expands, we must ask how this all adds up to a meaningful education for

PREDICTIONS

In five years . . .

Blended high-tech, hands-on school models in urban areas will leverage community resources, including employers, public transit, museums, theaters, and parks.

students. What about academic coherence? How will students make sense of a series of point solutions? Will a playlist of different and varied learning experiences add up to a powerful education? As someone who has spent the last decade advocating for small schools with a coherent core curriculum, I think these are important concerns. My advocacy for choice to the course level comes from a sense of urgency that we need to quickly expand access to quality options, particularly for students who have not been academically successful and particularly in gateway subjects such as math. The flip side of more choices will be an increased need for the sense-making functions of schools: guidance, application, and transcript management. Counselors and advisors supported by online guidance systems will play an increasingly important role. Projects constructed to build important habits of mind will be an important complement to personal skill-building online. Local opportunities to apply learning through internships and community service will remain important. And turning a variety of learning experiences into something that colleges will understand and value will grow in importance.

ARCHITECTURE OF ACHIEVEMENT

Unlike a traditional high school, you can't spot Carpe Diem Collegiate High School from the air—there's no football field or baseball diamond. From the street it looks more like a big box retail store than a school. From the front door, a visitor can see through the bullpen-style learning center into the surrounding glass-walled classrooms. Custom built, the architecture of the high-performing Yuma Arizona school supports the blended learning model by combining individual workstations with collaborative spaces. A respectful culture, blended curriculum, and open learning environment create a coherent school experience that works well for students and teachers.

Traditional architecture—a row of classrooms off a long hallway—has a dangerous gravity that encourages closed-door traditional practices in isolation. The basic building blocks of blended learning are communities not classrooms. Social learning makes it easy to create a project team that includes kids in the same room, in a state across the country, and in a country across the sea. An online curriculum that enables individual progress eliminates the basic assumptions around one teacher in a classroom with twenty-five students.

The new design characteristics for blended facilities are personalized, learning focused, collaborative, community connected, adaptable, and flexible. A blended school, based on these design principles, may design a series of learning experiences that require individual work, team projects, seminars, and advisory groups. As we saw with the design of Kunskapsskolan schools, the physical facility would require some big open spaces, some individual workstations, and some small- and medium-size group meeting rooms. The most important variable is flexibility—a reflection of the instructional vision but with room for change.

Blended models will generally have similar square footage requirements at the elementary level (but it's interesting to note that Rocketship builds schools for a fraction of the cost of surrounding districts). At the high school level, an online core curriculum makes it easy to consider a smaller part-time or double-shifted main facility with a fraction of the space and cost of a typical high school. A blended school schedule could include a day a week in partner locations such as a museum or theater and a day a week at an internship. A blended school could even spend a fair amount of time, for example, following a traveling drum and bugle corps (like a proposed school in Newark will do).

THE BLENDED FUTURE

As I mentioned at the beginning of this chapter, not only are we moving toward a majority of high school students in the United States doing the majority of their learning online, but also a high percentage of U.S. students will learn in schools that blend online and on-site instruction. A growing number of students will be home educated but more than 80 percent of parents will continue to appreciate the custodial value of schools and most students will enjoy the social aspects of school. Here is a detailed forecast of how the shift to blended learning will occur by the end of the decade, building on the chorus of "Old McDonald" using the mnemonic of N-E-I-E-I-O:

- *New:* The creation of new schools and conversion of existing charter schools to blended models will provide visible and important examples and will serve four million if a half a dozen networks develop real blended growth strategies.

- *Envelop:* The largest and most important change factor is that the whole calcified formal education system is being enveloped by an informal online learning system. Nearly all students will spend part of their day learning online at home or using smart phone applications.

- *Inject:* Where states allow it, students will take some of their courses online. This part-time enrollment will grow from three million students to about fifteen million students by 2020.

- *Extend:* Schools will extend the day and year using a personal digital playlist. Millions of elementary students will benefit from this inexpensive and effective strategy piloted by Rocketship Education.

- *Incorporate:* Most districts will incorporate blends of online learning to save money and boost learning. This is the most speculative prediction, but because half the districts say they're already working on this, thirteen to fifteen million students should be in district schools that incorporate an extensive amount of online learning by 2020.

- *Opt out:* The learning-at-home crowd (homeschooling plus virtual charter school enrollments) will triple from three to nine million students (or about 15 percent of K–12-age students).

If my predictions are wrong, they may prove to be too conservative rather than too ambitious. Ambient Insight's 2011 report indicated that online learning is larger and growing more rapidly than most observers estimated: "Over 4 million students are currently participating in some kind of formal virtual learning program. . . . The combined online population is currently growing by 46% a year and the growth rate is accelerating."[13] Although my projections are not quite as aggressive, at least two-thirds of U.S. students will be doing most of their learning online by 2020.

For generations we've sought quality at scale—good public schools in every neighborhood especially for low-income kids. The online learning providers are massively scalable and offer high levels of quality. There will soon be lots of capacity to support school models that blend online and on-site learning. Still, we don't want to underestimate the entrenched interests in the U.S. system of K–12 schooling. They have enormous influence over education policy. Are we going to craft policies that pave the way or stick with old ones that stand in the way? As you will see in Chapter Seven, the choice is ours.

INNOVATION

Policies That Will Make It Happen

Here's a frustrating thought experiment: with sixty days' notice, it would be logistically possible for a half dozen organizations (private companies and nonprofit groups) to make available to every student in the United States quality online high school math and science courses supported by effective instructors; they could also throw in twenty foreign languages—no problem. However, the U.S. history of local control makes this offer nearly inconceivable. If we don't address the United States' inability to innovate in the delivery of public services, it is certain that our children will be the first generation to be less well off than their parents.

Will your kids or grandkids have access to the best personal digital learning? The answer to that question depends a great deal on leadership. Since the mid-1990s, states have grabbed key policy levers to try and improve education—standards, assessment, data, accountability, and funding. With a push from the federal No Child Left Behind bill, states enacted elaborate outcome accountability systems and layered them on top of the input-driven programmatic funding for low-income students, special needs students, struggling readers, English language learners, and more. As a result, district budgets reflect a collection of special programs rather than a group of schools. Each program requires a manager and regular reports detailing participation. Efforts to hold schools accountable for results were just added to the old compliance system. It's frustrating for principals, many of whom are thinking, "Tell me what to do or hold me accountable for results, but not both."

A mountain of state and federal policy now sits on top of fourteen thousand school districts, most of which are trapped in a Gordian knot of bad policies and bad employment bargains. Unfortunately, U.S. education is saddled with a strange system of local control—it is anachronistic, ineffective for small districts, corrupt beyond repair in big districts, and antiquated by innovation. However, local control is embraced by strange bedfellows: employee groups that have learned to manipulate the system and conservatives that dislike the federal government. In an online global economy, allowing local school districts to monopolize educational offerings is an economic and civil rights disaster. The Byzantine three-tiered governance structure (local, state, and federal) is expensive, ineffective, and inequitable. The reason that U.S. families don't have access to quality is that our political system protects adults and traditions rather than doing what is best for children. The fix has been

POLICIES THAT WILL BOOST ACHIEVEMENT AND COMPLETION

- All students ready for college, careers, and citizenship
- All students are digital learners: 24/7 access to quality
- Choice to the course level: multiple statewide providers
- Fund kids not districts: portable need-based funding
- Show what you know: competency-based advancement
- The new deal: performance-based employment
- The good school promise: open good schools, close bad schools

impossibly difficult—until now. Personal digital learning allows us to rethink and re-create the delivery of public education—it reframes an old problem around a new opportunity.

READY FOR COLLEGE, CAREERS, AND CITIZENSHIP

Policy makers should begin with the goal of helping all students to graduate from high school ready for success in college, careers, and community service. The Common Core State Standards, introduced in 2010 and adopted by most states, was a good effort to define what students should know and be able to do in English and mathematics. Developed as a partnership between the nation's governors and the state education chiefs, the Common Core State Standards provides two primary benefits: real, coherent college-ready standards that will replace lower state standards and a big common content development platform. Since the mid-1990s curriculum developers have had to worry about aligning their products with fifty different state standards. The Common Core State Standards will make it easier for organizations to market online curricula, new platforms and tools, charter school models, and other learning innovations nationally. With less need to make adjustments for every state, there should be increased investment in content and tools—including open resources.

A benefit of the Common Core State Standards will be new testing schemes aligned with the standards that will be introduced by 2014. As part of the federal stimulus plan, two consortia representing forty-four states were awarded $365 million in October 2010. It is likely that they will produce tests that are better than what had been previously administered in most states, but they still may discourage an innovative curriculum. It's also not clear that assessments will be available on demand as is required by competency-based systems—that would lock in the old time-based system for another decade. As learning gets customized, assessment should be customized—reported against a common spine but reflective of a unique pathway.

College- and career-ready standards are the right starting point. This chapter goes on to outline a set of policies that support a "school-as-a-service" vision that will promote personal digital learning and will boost achievement and completion rates. The "as-a-service" notion comes from the world of computer software, but it is a way to think of education. Software as a service made it easier and cheaper to use computers, especially for those of us who use multiple devices; it's software on demand anytime, anywhere. It's no longer necessary to load computer programs with a disk; you can access almost any kind of program—spreadsheets, word processors, customer relationship managers, or tax preparation software—on the web. The emerging vision for education is school-as-a-service: a multiprovider service available on any device anytime, anywhere. The shift to school-as-a-service starts with a statewide commitment to every student as a digital learner.

ALL STUDENTS ARE DIGITAL LEARNERS

States should ensure that all students have an Internet access device and access to high-quality digital curriculum anytime, anywhere. This is a primary recommendation of *Digital Learning Now!*, a policy advisory issued December 2010 by the Foundation for Excellence in Education and chaired by former governors Jeb Bush and Bob Wise. For example, states could buy every student a laptop (like Maine did for secondary students) or tablet or netbook computer or the state could support a free or reduced price access device program for low-income students (similar to the federal lunch program). Students should be able to bring their own mobile devices to school. All students, or at least those who qualify for free and reduced price meals, should receive a tablet computer that allows them to access the core instructional materials anytime, anywhere there is broadband access. Combining textbook, supplemental materials, computer, and Title 1 funds, schools should be able to provide tablets loaded with a combination of free and premium content with some technical support and even a block of tutoring for less than they are currently spending across all these categories.

CHOICE TO THE COURSE LEVEL

Despite erected barriers, parents nationwide are exercising whatever options for better education they have available to them. More than half of U.S. parents already exercise educational choice according to Bruno Manno of the Walton Family Foundation:

> Policymakers continue to debate whether to expand or restrict the opportunity for all U.S. families to choose the K–12 schools their children will attend. Without fanfare, these families—especially low-income ones—have voiced their views. The result? A growing majority have voted with their feet to endorse school choice. Out of slightly more than 57 million K–12 students in the United States, nearly 52 percent, or almost 29.4 million, are enrolled in a K–12 school of choice.[1]

You hear about charter schools, homeschooling, and online learning, but Bruno points out that the biggest category of choice is the families representing nearly thirteen million students who move to gain access to better schools—the "real estate choice." The good news is that, with the expansion of online and blended learning, families won't have to move to gain access to quality education. Choice to the course level is another recommendation of *Digital Learning Now!*, which encouraged states to approve multiple statewide online learning providers, ensuring that they would be available to all students on a full- or part-time basis.

FUND KIDS NOT DISTRICTS

Reengineering school finance will prove to be the most contentious and technical challenge for state policy makers. Despite some state and federal equalization, school funding in the United States still reflects community wealth more than student need—we spend more on rich kids than poor kids. To boost the percentage of students who are college ready, states need a funding model that reflects student challenges rather than community wealth. That would require a statewide funding formula (called weighted student funding). Overriding strange local formulas and implementing a rational equalized formula will require a constitutional amendment in some states. A new funding formula would also create incentives for innovation, performance, course completion, and graduation.

School funding is a complicated mix of local, state, and federal investment. Local funding averages about a quarter of the total budget required but in some cities and states it can be more than half. Huge disparities exist where a high percentage of the budget comes from local funding and where school budgets are based largely on property taxes. A more conservative approach, equalized funding, is a step in the right direction. The State of Washington, for example, collects local receipts and redistributes a portion to even out funding between rich and poor communities. Weighted funding goes a step further and attempts to fund an appropriate amount for every student based on each student's challenges. Equalized and weighted funding are both politically difficult to adopt because they take money from affluent students and give it to low-income students. A public system premised on giving every student a shot at viable life options must reflect the level of challenge facing every student. Low-income children need more and we shouldn't be afraid to give it to them.

PREDICTIONS

In five years . . .

Several states will use performance contracting, charter schools being an example today, to authorize and manage the relationship with all schools and education providers.

In the United States, school districts control the budgets. Most principals have little discretionary authority. In several steps since the late 1980s years, U.K. education budgets were pushed to schools. Some U.S. districts have pushed a higher percentage of the budget to schools, but no state has a fully school-based budgeting system. Digital learning demands that states go a step further and push budgets to the students to enable choice to the course (and eventually to the lesson) level. A weighted formula may fund a high-need student at $12,000 and a low-need student at $6,000; the former would generate $2,000 per course and the latter $1,000 per course. This would create an incentive for providers to serve high-need students.

Weighted student funding is a big political challenge because it shifts money from wealthy communities to low-income students. Property taxes provide about half of education funding in the United States. Collecting them and redistributing them at the state level would require a constitutional amendment in many states and will be politically unpopular in most.

There are few communities in the United States that can guarantee every student a great teacher every year. Even if they could, the traditional school at its best does not work for some students. If we want every student to have a shot at college and careers, funding needs to reflect the challenges that individual students bring to school, not the wealth of the community. It should facilitate options and create incentives for achievement, completion, and innovation.

After the December 2010 release of *Digital Learning Now!* Utah and Florida legislatures followed major recommendations and proposed multiple statewide online learning providers and funding that followed students to the course level. In April 2011, the West Virginia Board of Education adopted all ten elements of high-quality digital learning. That should mean some version of money follows the student to the best course in about a half a dozen states by 2012. It won't be weighted and won't include incentives for serving high-need students, but it's a start.

SHOW WHAT YOU KNOW

The customized competency-based system described in Chapter Three requires a fundamentally different system architecture than an age- and time-based system. Our current system enrolls students by birthdays and assumes that they learn one year's worth of material in 180 days—kids ahead and behind are generally out of luck. The result is that struggling students or those who act out because they are bored are assigned to special education. A few fortunate students are assigned to gifted and talented classrooms and deemed worthy of rich art-infused curriculum in small classes that work ahead. This get-it-or-repeat-it system is a profoundly unjust, ineffective, and simply archaic way to structure education.

The new system will focus on learning rather than time. As we saw in Chapter Three, adaptive online assessments, rather than birthdays, will guide student placement. Units of study with multiple forms of assessment will guide student progress rather than an agrarian calendar. For example, thirteen grades could be replaced by five hundred badges. Most students would earn about forty badges each year. There would be no penalty for some students moving a little slower than others and students who are able to move faster would be free to do so.

Most states have seat-time requirements that require students to be in seats for 180 days per school year. Some have contact time requirements and class size requirements that lock in the old kids-in-rows age-cohort system. These must be replaced by matriculation systems in which students progress based on demonstrated mastery—they show what they know—on a regular basis and in which schools are free to use differentiated and distributed staffing (that is, different levels, groupings, and locations) strategies.

THE NEW DEAL

The old certification monopoly and back-loaded lockstep teacher compensation plans don't fit the exciting employment opportunities of the school-as-a-service future. New employment bargains will differentiate learning professionals by level, performance, and specialty. Teachers who add value and want more responsibility will be able to advance quickly, but pensions and benefits will be less lucrative than they were in the past.

The best possible physics teacher is probably not in your neighborhood. It is quite likely that if that teacher were available to teach online, he or she would not be able to teach your student. State certification laws and traditional budgets would prevent it. States have enacted elaborate certification laws that grant a preparation monopoly to teacher colleges—an expensive and time-consuming system that provides little benefit. States should scrap preparation requirements, remove barriers to teaching online, and remove class size limits that prohibit differentiated and alternative staffing models. Well-intentioned certification regimes would be beneficial in a handful of cases but an unnecessary barrier to teaching in most cases. If certification is required, it should be based on job performance—earned after a year or two of successfully boosting student achievement on the job as a teacher.

No Child Left Behind embraced the good teacher promise but it landed on a requirement for "highly qualified" teachers, a misplaced emphasis on certification that doesn't correlate strongly to performance. We need "highly effective" teachers, and now with digital learning, we need "highly effective learning experiences."

It wouldn't be too hard to create reciprocal agreements so that students had access to regional or national learning opportunities. For example, a high school student could take art and physical education locally, take economics and government at a community college, and take math and science at a statewide online school. Teresa Dove, an instructor at Florida Virtual School, won the first online learning teacher of the year award—she lives in western Virginia. Good thing Florida has a reciprocal certification agreement with Virginia. With a schedule built with support and guidance of a knowledgeable advisor, state funding should flow to each provider. Some of this exists in many places today but school districts actively discourage outside options to protect their budgets.

Certification (and tenure and paying for advanced degrees) doesn't seem to add much value, but to the extent it is used by states as a barrier to employment or recognition of performance over time, it should be reciprocal nationally so that good teachers can teach kids who need their help.

PREDICTIONS

In five years . . .

Fifty of the largest one hundred districts will, on a regular basis, close struggling schools and replace them with blended charter or contract schools, expand access to online courses, and embrace school networks.

We still have trouble predicting in the hiring process which teachers will be great, so the best we can do is have a two- or three-year provisional process resulting in certification for high-performing teachers. High Tech High is a high-performing network of nine schools in San Diego; their success formula starts with great teachers. They hire content-knowledgeable candidates and provide job-aligned preparation and support—that's probably the best strategy.

THE GOOD SCHOOL PROMISE

Accountability sounds punitive but it's really a promise that the public delivery system makes to families: "We promise you access to at least one good school and have reliable processes in place to make sure that's a reality."

An effective accountability process would authorize and support good schools, networks, and providers and would close bad schools and ineffective providers. Statewide school networks and online learning providers should be subjected to a rigorous review process that considers curriculum, instructional practices, and student outcomes. Course providers should demonstrate standards alignment and should be measured in completion rates and, when possible, student growth (requiring good pre- and postassessments). Results for full-time providers should be measured in terms of achievement (that is, students meeting standards) as well as student growth (academic gain over one year).

THE OPPOSITION

Maybe some of this sounds good to you, so you're wondering why this hasn't happened already. Beyond the weight of tradition—the collective weight of idealized remembrances of school—teachers unions, administrator associations, and school boards actively block online learning. Unions see this as loss of jobs and dues because online learning enables differentiated staffing models that may require fewer teachers per school, and distributed staffing (teaching remotely) is slowing, shifting a small percentage of employment to nonunion providers. Most districts consider state funding theirs and don't want to share, so they hate the idea of money following the student to the best option.

PREDICTIONS

In five years . . .

Budget woes will cause hundreds of districts and most charter networks to move to blended models, shifting to online instruction for a portion of the day to boost learning and operating productivity.

Online learning can quickly bring uniform quality to students statewide where policies allow. However, solid proposals for statewide virtual schools are routinely rejected. States construct ridiculous limitations such as bounding the Internet by district or county or limiting the size of virtual schools. Given that some of the largest online learning providers are private companies, arguments of profiteering can mask the main issue— protecting public-sector jobs.

Some people are concerned about profits being generated by companies supporting the public education system but private companies are routinely engaged in every other public delivery system—health, transportation, energy, and defense. The government contracts with private providers because they bring innovation, scale, and flexibility to the task. For two generations, in fact, private companies have essentially been in charge of a large part of education: textbooks, technology, tutoring, and testing—a roughly $25 billion sector. Employee group resistance grows as companies take on instructional and school management roles. The question is not the tax status of the entity but whether they have the ability to meet particular needs. Private companies have incentives for speed, quality, and scale that government entities don't share; they should be engaged when those benefits can benefit society.

The combination of tradition, bureaucracy, and protectionism stifles innovation and investment and is why the sector is more than a decade behind. Engagement tools common in games and productivity tools that have long been common in business, for example, are just now being introduced into schools. School districts and employee groups may have successfully dampened charter school expansion for more than a decade, and even though they can't stop the spread of and investment in online learning, what they can do is make it more difficult to make these options available to students

Public education is a promise to U.S. families, not tenure for school districts. We should publicly fund the best possible education for every student. If a nonprofit or private company can run a better school for less than a government agency why wouldn't we want to make that option available to parents? The answer often comes down to competing worldviews.

THE VALUES WAR

Such political skirmishes are the visible signs but there is a war of competing values under way. Canadian writer Jane Jacobs came to understand this about cities. Her primary interest was

JANE JACOBS'S SYSTEMS
OF SURVIVAL (PARTIAL LIST)

Guardian Moral Syndrome	Commerce Syndrome
Shun trading	Shun force
Exert prowess	Compete
Be obedient and disciplined	Be efficient
Adhere to tradition	Be open to inventiveness and novelty
Respect hierarchy	Use initiative and enterprise
Be loyal	Come to voluntary agreement
Dispense largesse	Invest for productive purposes
Be exclusive	Collaborate easily with strangers and aliens
Be fatalistic	Be optimistic
Treasure honor	Be honest

urban planning and decay. She is best know for her 1961 book *The Death and Life of Great American Cities* (a title that Diane Ravitch ironically appropriated for her 2010 personal reversal and defense of the status quo, *The Death and Life of the Great American School System*) and killing a Manhattan expressway. But she was most proud of figuring out the key to economic expansion. The cultural value system described by Jacobs as the Guardian Moral Syndrome is an even better description of public education than of public works.[2] Now common in public delivery systems, the Machiavellian Guardian Moral Syndrome is based on loyalty and hierarchy; it "shuns trading" and adheres to tradition. The alternative commerce system values competition, initiative, and inventiveness.

Fifty years later, it's uncanny how closely Jane's guardian value system resembles many urban school systems. Efforts to inject values of commerce into public education are attacked as privatization. These attacks are aimed at private management of schools but in most cases these are not for-profit organizations, they are nonprofit ones like Teach For America (TFA), New School Venture Fund, and KIPP—operating with values foreign and threatening to guardians. This is an important distinction—it's not the profit motive, it's an improvement mindset that is fundamentally different. The four hundred nonprofit reform organizations that I've had a chance to work with were part of what Jane called the Commerce Syndrome. Few of them ran surpluses but they were all about openness, innovation, and collaboration. By contrast, many of the dozens of districts that I worked with were clearly guardians (or quickly reverted to guardians after interloping "commerce" superintendents were fired)—they were all about hierarchy, tradition, and exclusivity. The difference is governance: political leadership creates guardians; mission-focused perpetual governance creates a commerce mentality.

The Internet doesn't conform well to guardian protocols; it is by nature open to inventiveness and novelty. This explains some of the resistance to online learning; it just doesn't fit the boundaries of tradition and the practices of the past. An effective twenty-first-century public delivery system needs the values of commerce with a mission of equity and excellence. That doesn't require a privatized system but it does demand a responsive and accountable system.

TRANSFORMATIONAL PRODUCTIVITY

We can end this policy discussion on an optimistic note by pointing to signs of leadership. After the midterm elections, Secretary of Education Arne Duncan gave an important speech about productivity that received little attention.[3] Duncan began outlining the "new normal" (appropriating a phrase from bond giant Pimco's Mohamed El-Erian, who predicted a post-financial-crisis world of lower investment returns). The secretary urged that an extended period of time with persistently low tax revenues was a call for educational productivity—a time to do more with less. Duncan pleaded not to cut back days, instructional time, art, physical education, and languages, and not to lay off talented new teachers. The remarkable part of Duncan's speech was his case for "transformational change" and rethinking "structure and delivery," and his call to "explore productive alternatives." This was the first time a U.S. education secretary recognized the potential for "transformational productivity," the first time a secretary attacked the basic system architecture as "a century-old factory model—the wrong model for the twenty-first century." Duncan railed against seat-time requirements, antiquated compensation systems, and inequitable school finance. He called for the smart use of technology—a potential "force multiplier"—online tools and virtual schools. It wasn't a compelling vision but it was a call to action. Duncan said, "The new normal can be a wake-up call."

Now that anyone can learn anything, anywhere, except for where prohibited by state policy, it's time to rethink how we provide public education in America. State leaders, in particular, have the historic responsibility to guide the pivot from books to digital content, from bubble sheet tests to instant feedback, from birthdays to competency-based progress, from funding school inputs to funding student outcomes, and from back-loaded employment to diverse performance-based learning professions.

States should approve multiple statewide online learning providers. School districts should incorporate online learning into new blended formats that personalize learning and allow students to progress based on demonstrated competence. Students and families deserve high-quality choices—now. A majority of U.S. parents already exercise choice. It's time for state policies to reflect parent demand and educational opportunity. It's time to make educational choice the norm not the exception.

Our public policy should promote productivity not protectionism; our public policy should promote nimble delivery not a rigid one-size-fits-few system; our public policy should be about cost-effective options not a bureaucratic monopoly. In short, education policy should be about kids not adults. That said, improved ability to meet student needs and expanded and enhanced employment options for teachers and other learning professionals paint an exciting picture of the future.

INVESTMENT

Paying for Innovation

Education is a vital public service and the basis for long-term economic development. However, it operates largely like it did one hundred years ago with same-age groups of kids slogging through a print curriculum. We've added more tests and struggle to use the few data elements we have to drive improvement. But improving the old system won't produce the learning outcomes that modern society demands. It will take new engaging models of personalized digital learning incorporating multiple pathways to support college and career readiness, to promote college completion and advanced job certification, and to encourage lifelong learning.

Fortunately, at least in the United States, where we spend more than anyone else (except Luxemburg), we can do better for less, but the new tools and new schools will take large capital investments. Government spending, foundation grants, and private equity investments all come with particular advantages and limitations. Big advances will require that we make smart investments. But who should be investing and how? As you will see in this chapter each sector that is poised to invest in learning—public, nonprofit, and private—brings its own set of limitations and benefits. What is clear, however, is that no one sector can do it alone. Consider, for example, how former president Clinton was able to work with heads of state and the pharmaceutical industry to address the AIDS crisis in Africa. By negotiating big purchase commitments from a number of African countries, Clinton was able to purchase AZT, an HIV treatment regime, at a very low cost. He created a market where it had not existed. He combined public leadership and philanthropic support to marshal market forces for good. This is the kind of thinking that we need to bring to the problem of our schools.

THE FEAR AND PROMISE OF PRIVATE CAPITAL

There is a historical acceptance of private-sector generation of textbooks, testing, tutoring, and technology in U.S. K–12 education—a 5 percent sliver of the $600 million segment of the U.S. economy. It's the move from vendor to operator that really raises opposition. Edison, a profit-seeking education management company, was formed with a flourish in the 1990s and it took on the operation of district and charter schools. Encouraged by gubernatorial enthusiasm, Edison took on too much too fast and the quality of their results suffered. Their public struggles created widespread resentment and probably set back private-sector contributions by a decade. Almost two decades later, several for-profit charter school networks including National Heritage Academies, Charter Schools USA, Mosaica Education, and The Leona Group, L.L.C. have quietly built substantial regional chains and are now larger than their nonprofit counterparts. Online learning providers including K^{12}, Connections Academy, Apex Learning, and a handful of other for-profit providers will probably top $1 billion in revenue by 2012. The growth of for-profit school operators and online providers comes in the face of vitriolic opposition from public employee groups.

Private capital has inherent incentives for speed, quality, and scale. Market pressures of competition drive service improvement. Investors' expectation of a return on capital drives marketing and sales efforts. Compared to nonprofits, private enterprise can often hire a more talented and experienced team to attack an opportunity because of the potential for future financial reward. Another advantage of real innovation capital is the ability to follow a good idea to a better idea. With a grant, you may get what was proposed whether good or bad. Venture capital follows great ideas and often ends up funding something different and better than was originally proposed.

NONPROFIT LIMITATIONS

Teach For America (TFA) and charter school network KIPP are terrific nonprofit organizations—darlings of the foundation world and recipients of giant federal grants. But after twenty years, TFA places a tenth of a percent of U.S. teachers and KIPP serves five-hundredths of a percent of U.S. students.

They both require huge philanthropic and federal commitments annually just to maintain operations, much less grow. They are the best of the best of the nonprofit sector but they are not scalable or sustainable.

Nonprofit organizations receive tax-exempt status for serving the public good. They operate on individual donations and foundation grants, and occasionally earn fee income. Most foundations support specific projects with restricted grants rather than providing unrestricted scaling capital. Foundations increasingly develop an investment strategy that follows a "theory of action" and few nonprofits fit neatly into these impact strategies. That's not bad, but it does make it harder for nonprofits to raise money, particularly unrestricted grants. It means that nonprofits have to shoehorn their requests to meet the guidelines of a few foundations that might be interested. For example, a charter school developer in Tennessee who needs $3 million to expand can go to one or two local foundations or one or two national foundations that may have Tennessee on their target list—a very short list of potential funders. If the local funders don't like charters or the national funders don't like Tennessee, the developer may be out of luck for growth capital.

It's not like nonprofit school developers, reform advocates, and software developers can go to the bank and get funding— it's even harder for nonprofits to get access to traditional debt financing because they don't have much of a balance sheet and have uncertain revenue streams. Some big nonprofits like American Institutes for Research and ETS have a high percentage of income earned from big government testing or research contracts but for most nonprofits it's really hard to grow and sustain operations. With a big annual fundraising requirement, nonprofit organizations are always at risk of a key funder changing its theory of action and being left high and dry.

With foundation support, an army of management consultants from The Bridgespan Group, McKinsey & Company, and The Parthenon Group are trying to help nonprofits expand their impact and become less reliant on grants and donations by encouraging the adoption of business models that include more earned income such as fee-for-service work. But nonprofit organizations have limitations. They lack the incentives for speed, quality, and scale inherent in return-seeking capital. Growing a nonprofit may expand impact, but the director's passion for the mission must be stronger than the headaches associated with growth because the compensation is not likely to substantially change with scale.

PREDICTIONS

In ten years . . .

Despite generally flat funding for education, the U.S. K–12 instructional materials and related technologies market will grow by more than 50 percent—an explosion of digital services will offset the decline of print.

Nonprofit school improvement groups and school development networks are making a difference in small ways but are reliant on local funders committed to the community or on one of the national funders with a current focus on their line of expertise. School reform advocates can occasionally make a big impact with a focused effort but going up against the interests of the status quo often requires a big long-term commitment. Nonprofits are central to foundation strategies that all envision massive social benefit, but given the inherit limitation, we simply cannot rely on the nonprofit sector alone to help achieve the transformation of U.S. public education.

In addition to trouble with scaling, nonprofits aren't built to innovate. They have weak incentives to improve productivity; a better way to serve their mission may result in a larger year-end surplus but links to personal performance incentives are likely to be absent or weak. Nonprofits have a limited ability to aggregate risk capital, place risky bets, kill projects that aren't working (because of promises to foundations), and support promising projects with a follow-through on investments. Nonprofits meet pressing charitable needs in U.S. society. Compared to other countries, U.S. nonprofit organizations are supported by a generous level of philanthropic support. But they are just not very good at innovating or scaling. That's what private enterprise was created to do.

SCHOOL DISTRICT LIMITATIONS

School districts aren't well suited to produce or scale innovation either. They don't have the ability to raise investment capital (other than grants or construction bonds), most don't do capital budgeting, and they have weak incentives to invest for productivity improvement. Schools usually get paid based on the number of students, not on results. Most districts, funded by local and state taxes, have a use-it-or-lose-it budget, so when they do save some money during the year there is a rush to spend it all before the end of the year. Some schools get paid on an October count, so there's no incentive to keep kids in school all year.

Innovation typically requires the ability to accumulate and invest risk capital, produce a productivity-improving tool and capture associated intellectual property, and produce a return on investment by marketing or selling the resulting product or service. Districts were not organized for these purposes. School districts also have little internal capacity for improvement. They are organized to manage programs not projects. Federal, state, and philanthropic grants given directly to districts have failed to yield substantial academic improvement. Promising efforts are usually swept away by revolving-door leadership.

PREDICTIONS

In ten years . . .

More than $10 billion in school facilities will be sold for redevelopment because major remodels of antiquated buildings will become cost prohibitive.

How can we combat these weak incentives for improvement and scale? The feds tried fear. For the last decade of U.S. education, the federal government attempted to impose a system of humiliation and progressive intervention (that I supported as an attempt to deal with chronic failure). Lame state implementations and muted consequences led to little improvement. There are clearly limits to how much you can get out of a purely punitive system but it does seem clear that there must be a consequence of going out of business for failing to educate children—bad schools don't deserve tenure.

THE RIGHT CAPITAL FOR THE JOB

Each of the sectors—public, nonprofit, and private—has strengths and weaknesses that it brings to the challenge of innovating education. A public delivery system may be good at promoting social equity but it's not well suited to produce excellence; a public delivery system may produce consistency but it almost never produces innovation. Philanthropic and private investments have the potential to offset some of the shortcomings of public delivery systems. In trying to determine how they each can contribute, it is useful to consider their traditional roles, which are shown in the table.

Seed funding gets an organization started. In the private sector the early investors, or "angels," are often friends and family who purchase common stock. Venture capital investors may invest a bit later but well before the business model has been proved and potentially before operations have commenced

The Role for Philanthropic and Private Capital[1]

Dimension	Public Delivery	Nonprofit	For-Profit
Seed	Authorization and appropriation	Grants and donations	Angel and venture investors
Operating	Authorization and appropriation	Donations, service fees (occasional)	Sales and profits
Scaling	Authorization and appropriation	Grants, usually project specific	Private equity
Advantages	Coverage and equity	Targeting vulnerable populations	Efficiency and scale
Limitations	Flexibility and responsiveness	Scale and sustainability	Unlikely to target unprofitable markets

("prerevenue"). They typically buy preferred stock, which provides some liquidation preferences, and because of the risk involved often target a return of six to ten times their investment over five to seven years.

Although initially drawing on contributed capital, for-profit companies rely on sales and profits to fund operations. For-profit companies target the most profitable market segments and are less likely, without foundation support, to meet the needs of vulnerable youth. Foundations can mitigate risk, aggregate demand, or subsidize returns to make underserved markets more attractive for private operators.

BLENDED CAPITAL IS COMMON

The U.S. education sector bias and related legal prohibitions against investment by private companies are remarkable in contrast to other public delivery systems. Innovations in health care, energy production and transmission, and transportation are often the product of private investment in government-requested, -sponsored, or -incentivized projects. Scalable solutions with a business model are required across the U.S. sector and across the globe to promote equity and excellence.

The clean-energy sector is an example of how government and private capital have collaboratively funded innovation. The *Wall Street Journal* recently reported, "The US government doled out $502 million for a dozen wind and solar energy projects."[2] The big winner was Iberdrola Renewables, a Spanish wind giant. Coming in second was Horizon, a subsidiary of a Portuguese firm. Third place went to a U.K.-owned firm. These grants will likely result in an energy-efficient infrastructure, but it's interesting to note that the big winners were all foreign owned, an indication of where public incentives have encouraged private investment over the last decade, and all the grant recipients were for-profit companies. The government will follow up these grants with $4 billion in grants for companies promising to build out a smart grid and improve power efficiency.[3]

Clean-tech investments have been driven by government incentives as well as the expectation that a healthy marketplace is being developed. Kleiner Perkins Caufield & Byers and Khosla Ventures have billion-dollar funds focused on clean tech. Scores of midsize funds like MissionPoint Capital Partners are drafting the leaders. Capital flow in the clean-tech sectors has been a result of positive trends in people, technology, markets, and policy. More talented entrepreneurs are focused on solving problems associated with global warming and the need for alternative energy sources. There is also an ongoing shift in consumer behavior and public sentiment. Government is providing incentives not only to create these kinds of businesses, but also for potential customers to buy these types of products. Advancements in control systems, alternative energy sources, batteries, and smart devices are accelerated by competition to find solutions to problems created by rising energy prices, geopolitical risk, and global warming. Innovation is being funded by entrepreneurs, research investment, and venture capitalists encouraged by government subsidies. The $3 billion quickly assembled and put to work by the private sector to promote clean energy are an example of the mobilization and leverage governments can expect when they create space for public-private partnerships.

In the 1970s, energy production and transmission were largely a function of public utilities. Today, the market is becoming diversified and dynamic in large part because of public incentives and investments. K–12 schooling is an inefficient public delivery system incapable of achieving desired outcomes or supporting necessary innovations. As with clean-tech industries (defense, health, transportation, and energy), the federal government should invite rather than ban private-sector participation in the nation's education agenda. Unfortunately, just the opposite is happening. The Department of Education, directed by language from Congress, did not invest any of the $100 billion stimulus in private enterprise. About 90 percent of the stimulus was spent to save existing jobs. The roughly $10 billion in incentive grants barred private enterprises from requesting grants (but they were allowed to subcontract to a nonprofit). Despite President Obama's rhetoric about innovation, his administration has made only weak attempts to encourage private participation in educational improvement.

OPPORTUNITIES FOR PRIVATE INVESTMENT

Expansion of broadband and reduction in the price of access devices and powerful application development platforms—all primarily a result of private investment—have changed the learning opportunity set. Equally exciting is the development of social entrepreneurship—impact-oriented enterprises with a return-seeking or at least sustainable business model. Nobel Prize winner Muhammad Yunus, founder and manager of micro-finance pioneer Grameen Bank, popularized this idea that a business approach is often the best way to meet a large need. Social enterprises (both nonprofit and for-profit) are being advanced by groups like Echoing Green in clean tech, and Startl, New Profit, and NewSchools Venture Fund in education.

The worldwide recession accelerated the instincts of and opportunities for the millennial generation to do meaningful work. The number of applications to Teach For America,

Education Pioneers, and Eli Broad's Fellows program all continue to grow. It's encouraging that big education conferences are being hosted by Yale business students and that education innovation incubators are popping up around the country. Talent is being attracted to problems in global education with the expansion of additional educational career options. As a venture capital investor, I see how the significant increase in the quantity and quality of proposals makes it easier to seek high impact and high return. In other words, the world of learning and education is opening up great opportunities for investors. I see five main categories:

1. *Digital content,* particularly curriculum that adapts to individual learning needs, learning games, simulations, and virtual environments. Open resources will continue to play an expanded role but there will be a strong market for premium content because of the following:
   - It has embedded assessment and achievement analytics similar to Mangahigh's.
   - It offers a curated series like Pearson's Common Core–aligned *digits.*
   - It proposes a proved library of high school courses such as those offered by Apex Learning.
   - It is part of a comprehensive curriculum on a school management platform such as Connexus from Connections Learning.

2. *Online learning* where curriculum and instruction are provided online. Full- and part-time enrollment in online learning will continue to double every three years with most of the growth from for-profit providers who are able to work nationally but tailor services locally. An expanding category of online learning will be remote teachers providing

speech therapy and other special needs, language acquisition, Advanced Placement and other college credit courses, higher-level math, and science and technology (STEM) courses. These distributed workforce models make high-quality services available on demand; they are cheaper for districts, often better for students, and provide great flexibility for teachers.

3. *Blended learning* school development and improvement. Innovative school models that incorporate the best of online and on-site learning will expand as new school networks and will be adopted by struggling schools. Private-sector participants will operate schools and provide services to nonprofit and public school operators. There will be lots of nonprofit providers but private-sector participants with a stronger balance sheet will be better equipped to support a comprehensive change process.

4. *Learning platforms* will customize pathways through digital content libraries based on comprehensive student profiles, teachers will benefit from instructional and management tools, and students will appreciate social learning features. Although foundations are attempting to build an uberplatform, private enterprise will continue to innovate spurred by viral growth of social platforms like Edmodo and application marketplaces like Google and Apple have launched.

5. *Aligned services* that support student, teacher, and school success. Closely coupled learning platforms will be online tutoring, professional development, data analysis, operational support, and other school improvement services. Wireless Generation, recently sold to News Corporations, developed their own assessment (mCLASS) and professional development services and won big contracts to help districts build aligned instructional systems.

These five categories will require billions of dollars of investment in research and development. They will require skilled teams with incentives to produce and scale innovation. But in every case, these categories of innovation will require public leadership to create room to pilot and they will require foundations to mitigate risk and promote equity. With all the new venture capital and private equity interested in learning, it is a great time for state and urban leaders to invite the private sector to spend money solving their education problem. An American Enterprise Institute for Public Policy Research report stated that "[c]oordinated public-private partnerships will be key to meeting the unique challenge of rapidly scaling access to quality education. Private investment will not fix the problems with education, but it will not be fixed without it."[4]

PREDICTIONS

In one year . . .

Common Core State Standards will spark a new wave of venture and philanthropic investment in digital content, resulting in engaging and innovative adaptive content libraries and mobile apps.

Somewhat looser than a formal partnership is a blended capital ecosystem in which governments create spaces where philanthropic and private capital can innovate. India serves as an example; there is simply no way the government can scale quality public education fast enough to meet the needs of the half-billion students. Foundations and private operators have stepped in to meet the requirements of the least well-served students.

BLENDED CAPITAL ECOSYSTEM IN INDIA

In some Indian urban centers more than half of the students attend low-cost private schools. What began as an underground education system is, in some states, expanding and becoming a recognized web of choice through the work of philanthropic and private investment.

In some cases, private and philanthropic efforts are well coordinated. For example, Indian School Finance Company (ISFC) provides small loans to low-cost school operators for expanding and improving the quality of their school. Loans are often made to schools rated by Gray Matters Capital, an operating foundation that developed a rating system to promote quality. These efforts are complemented by an emerging advocacy sector including grant-funded groups such as Centre for Civil Society, run by University of Michigan–trained economist Parth Shah, advancing quality educational options for the poor.

Dasra, mentioned in Chapter One, is a grant-funded social enterprise incubator in Mumbai. With the support of the emerging Indian philanthropic sector, each year Dasra helps a dozen educational entrepreneurs develop a business plan and a support network as part of a larger cohort of change makers.

Educomp Solutions, the Indian market leader in education services, operates three branded private school networks in the low-, medium-, and high-price ranges, as well as providing education technology services to government schools. With support from the Michael & Susan Dell Foundation, Educomp is supporting education technology pilots in low-cost private schools. Similarly, the American Indian Foundation supports the Digital Equalizer program, an effort to bridge the digital divide and achievement gap.

Another fascinating aspect of the affordable private school space in India is the variety of private operators driven by a mixture of employee need, social responsibility, and market opportunity. SKS Microfinance, the leader in microfinance, retailer Fabindia, and steel maker Usha Martin all operate networks of schools. Career Launcher operates K–12 schools and provides test preparation and career education. Aptech provides career education and, like Career Launcher, earns about $40 million in revenue.

Newcastle University professor James Tooley, author most recently of *The Beautiful Tree,* also deserves a good deal of credit for advancing affordable private schools in India, as well as in China and Africa, and for promoting promising school models and return-seeking investments. Tooley founded Empathy Learning Systems, which operates and supports low-cost schools. Next, he plans to connect a group of regional school operators into a super network for efficiency and sustainability.

The historical bias against and restrictions placed on private-sector involvement in U.S. education is odd and counter-productive. U.S. challenges are different than Indian challenges but encouraging private sector investment in learning innovation is just as important to meeting national educational goals.

We're not likely to see the likes of Microsoft running affordable private schools in the United States, but like with England's academies, we could see—with a little encouragement—more corporations sponsoring and partnering with government schools. Amgen has been instrumental in supporting high school improvement in Los Angeles. Citigroup has supported a national network of career academies for almost thirty years.

IBM is partnering with New York City on a high school that will train computer technicians—and after grade 14, they will be first in line for jobs at IBM.

Arizona is the only state to allow for-profit charter operators (in all other states, private operators must contract with nonprofit charter holders). There would certainly be more operators and more investment in innovative school models if it were not so difficult to get a charter and open a school and so easy to get kicked out of a charter that cost $300,000 to develop (and about $10 million if a building is developed specifically for the school).

PHILANTHROPY'S NICHE

Foundations have, or should have, two distinct competencies compared to private enterprise and the public sector. First, they can take the long view. Markets drive an obsession with quarterly results for public companies and eager investors can encourage start-up companies to look for quick wins. Unfortunately, the public sector is also becoming myopic with a focus on fundraising for the next election. Congressional votes are increasingly polarized and it is becoming more difficult to deal with long-term structural problems. Because most foundations assume perpetual operations, they have a built-in advantage of taking the long view. The ability to take a generational view rather than a quarterly view makes foundations a useful part of public-private partnerships.

Foundations are also uniquely well suited to promote equity of opportunity. Although private enterprises are obligated by their fiduciary responsibility to shareholders to attack the most attractive market segments, foundations can focus on the least well served in society. Scholarship programs are a classic case of philanthropy extending access to a private university. Afford-able housing is an example of a category in which government incentives and philanthropic support have marshaled private investment to create communities that work for a variety of income levels. Public health is another example of how phil-anthropic support is key to covering uninsured patients in the United States and extending access to basic care in the develop-ing world.

Here are three specific actions that foundations could do to leverage their equity-seeking investments with a long-term per-spective for K–12 education:

- Provide a promising new consumer learning product, such as an online guidance and tutoring platform, to low-income households with the goal of eventually having public subsidies. This would extend the learning day, help students make better choices, and make them more successful at school.

- Bring key partners together to create new important capabilities such as developing a learning platform and investing enough in the development of the product (or the market) to attract significant partner investments. Big libraries of adaptive content and smart recommendation engines will be expensive and foundation involvement can be the necessary catalyst for other partners to align efforts.

- Advocating for improved public policy can be risky and expensive but it can be the most highly leveraged philanthropy—a few hundred thousand dollars well targeted can move hundreds of millions of public money. Advocating for student access to full- and part-time online learning is a key entry point to a performance-based, multiprovider education system. When the advocacy is successful, millions will be invested and low-income students will be able to access quality courses and instruction.

As an example of the last bullet, The Foundation for Excellence in Education sponsored the Digital Learning Council, chaired by former governors Jeb Bush and Bob Wise, which is an example of a rapid virtual nonpartisan policy development process. Over the course of three months, about one hundred leading executives, policy analysts, technologists, policy makers, and education leaders collaborated online to develop a recommended state policy platform for digital learning. One sponsor called the resulting report, *Digital Learning Now!,* the "constitution for the revolution."[5]

IMPACT INVESTING

Impact investors combine the profit-seeking behavior of private equity investors with the impact-seeking goals of philanthropy. For the first time, the flow of proposals from high-quality teams is strong enough that investors can expect high social returns *and* market rate returns. City Light Capital is a New York City venture fund charting the course in a new category of funds called *impact investing*. In areas such as education, public safety, and clean technology, City Light has a high bar for return and social benefit. Founder and managing director Josh Cohen said, "We measure our success as investors by the financial returns we achieve and the impact our companies create through improvements in the ways we protect people, property and places, educate and inform ourselves, and consume energy and environmental resources, while promoting an open society."[6]

Foundations receiving tax-exempt status in the United States are required to donate at least 5 percent of their assets on an annual basis. To advance their philanthropic mission, foundations cull through grant requests to find the right investments for their required distribution. It is unfortunate that foundations pay so much attention to the 5 percent of their assets that they give away and so little attention to the other 95 percent—they should be putting at least a portion of their endowment to work to advance their mission. Impact investing is a significant innovation for philanthropy because it can drive impact out of endowment investments, not just grant making.

Given the likelihood of scaled social benefit from impact investing it will become commonplace for foundations to invest a portion of their endowment in mission-related investments. Many foundations will also become more active in providing venture debt and credit enhancements to return-seeking enterprises. The W. K. Kellogg Foundation devoted $100 million of its endowment to mission-related investments: "We supplement our grantmaking with mission-driven investments that enable high-impact financial institutions to move capital into vulnerable communities." For at least a portion of their endowment, Kellogg looks for a social and financial return on investment.[7] And they are not alone; other foundations are investing in venture funds and return-seeking vehicles with social ends. States, pension funds, and universities will all add impact funds to their endowments because it has become clear that education is one sector in which it is possible to build a scalable business and create a significant impact.

If just a few of the larger national foundations focused just 5 percent of their endowments on mission-related investments (funds and direct investments) rather than random mutual funds, there could be an order of magnitude increase in investment in learning innovation.

NEWSCHOOLS VENTURE FUND—IMPACT INVESTING EMERGES

NewSchools Venture Fund, a nonprofit organization in San Francisco, is supported by foundation grants. They are inching foundations closer to the kind of impact investing described previously. Like any venture fund, they raise and invest money. But NewSchools' primary mission is transforming public education. For the most part, NewSchools takes big grants from foundations and turns around and makes small grants to edupreneurs (educational entrepreneurs) who get some useful advice and networking. NewSchools makes occasional return-seeking investments when there is clear mission alignment. Founder Kim Smith said, "We have supported a number of terrific entrepreneurs who are building great companies, including Acelero Learning, Revolution Foods, Wireless Generation, Teachscape, and a few that are getting up and running." Kim sees education becoming more palatable for investors. "Technology advances are bringing down the cost of doing business, forthcoming Common Core State Standards and assessments are making it more possible and cost-effective to develop and scale new products, parents are really interested in technology tools that help them personalize and customize learning for students, and new teachers and administrators are looking for technology tools that improve their own productivity."[8] Charter School Growth Fund, another nonprofit venture fund, owns DreamBox, a return-seeking K–3 adaptive math product.

There will always be those out to make a buck at the expense of others, but there is an expanding opportunity set to promote social benefit and produce market returns. Private enterprise is uniquely well suited to produce and spread learning applications and, as a result, will be an important partner for public systems in the learning revolution worldwide.

GOOD GOVERNMENT

Governors, state chiefs, and big city superintendents can do a lot to create an innovation ecosystem that leverages public, private, and philanthropic support. By aggregating demand and creating room to try, public leaders can effectively invite philanthropic and private capital to solve their problems. The best example is the New York City iZone, a planned network of two hundred schools that will quickly deploy existing online learning systems and another two hundred schools that will pilot the next generation of engaging and adaptive learning experiences.

The Recovery School District in post-Katrina New Orleans is another example of a public innovation space that encouraged charter school development (but little significant private-sector involvement). Florida created statewide access to online courses on a part-time basis with rolling enrollment and performance payment (full payment when a student successfully completes a course). Utah went a step further and opened up personal choice to the course level with multiple statewide providers. The transformation to personal digital learning will require state and district leaders to create safe spaces to innovate. Partnerships with foundations and research firms around these public innovation zones will produce new knowledge and spur interest and investment.

The Indian government has aggressive plans to marshal the power of venture capital to produce and scale learning innovations. Although their plans may be smaller than the stimulus-related grant programs announced by the Obama administration, they may prove to have an even bigger impact given their embrace of private investment strategies.

In fall 2010, I met with Saurabh Srivastava, cofounder of the National Association of Software and Service Companies in India and godfather of Indian angel and venture investing (a community of investors in start-up companies using a recognized set of terms and conditions). As a member of the prime minister's Innovation Council, Saurabh is developing a $1 billion innovation fund. Chair of the Innovation Council is Sam Pitroda—an intense and brilliant Chicago-based veteran entrepreneur who advises the prime minister on information and infrastructure. They have seen mobile phone use grow from two million handsets in 2000 to 846 million by March of 2011,[9] and they intend to make educational use of accelerating connectivity. In contrast to the U.S. political food-fight, India's leadership is laying the groundwork for the innovation economy—they are smart, focused, and optimistic.

EMPLOYMENT

Changing Our Job Descriptions

Personal digital learning won't just change the experience of students in K–12 education, it will fundamentally change the lives and work of those people who are in any way engaged in supporting and educating children. New pathways to learning are expanding the number of jobs and the type of jobs that promote learning; at the same time, innovations in learning technology are creating more opportunities for edupreneurs to create new tools and schools.

The notion of "educator" has come unmoored from its previous definitions and associations. It is floating free just waiting to be grabbed up and inhabited by entrepreneurs like super tutor Sal Khan or learning game developer Toby Rowland of Mangahigh or Nic Borg of social learning platform Edmodo and other smart, imaginative individuals who didn't necessarily set out to make careers in education but who ended up there nevertheless because of one thing: the Internet. Without You-Tube, the math lessons that Khan created for his niece would have become a nice family story, a pleasant memory, a few letters stuffed in an old notebook, not a career-changing and world-changing enterprise. Without success in casual games, it's not likely that Rowland would have attempted to build learning games. Without connecting with friends on Facebook and then on Twitter, Borg wouldn't have gained the insight to launch a social learning platform. We know the Internet is powerful. What we need to look at now is exactly how this will shape new roles, opportunities, and responsibilities for all of us.

PARENTS AS EDUCATORS

Traditional schools have a love-hate relationship with parents. They know that parental involvement is the key to successful students. Many schools thrive on the efforts of fundraising parents and they worry about and complain about the parents who don't have the time to support students at home to make sure they come to school on time, homework completed, ready to learn. But it is the rare administrator or teacher who welcomes parental feedback on curriculum or methods. The classroom is their domain. The rise of personal digital learning is changing these relationships. Students and parents are finding new ways to learn on their own.

Parents have always been the primary educators of their children but as the boundary between school and home fades parents will be asked to play a larger role in the formal education of their children—and teachers will need to let them in. What about those parents who don't have the education, the free time, or the emotional or financial stability to focus on their child's education? Fortunately, as we saw in Chapter Five, an education based on personal digital learning has the power to bring a world of supportive adults and peers into the life of a student. For those parents who are involved or want to be involved, the opportunities to shape their children's education—from homeschooling to creating virtual schools, for example—are evolving rapidly.

About 3.5 million K–12 students in the United States learn at home between homeschooling and virtual charter schools. Options are expanding and quality is improving. For many parents, who previously may not have considered homeschooling, online curricula offered by organizations such as K^{12} (profiled in Chapter Six) may make having their children learn at home a possibility. This is especially true for parents of students who are struggling in school or have health issues that make attending school difficult. Parents of students with learning disabilities, for example, often find that managing the connection with teachers, specialists, the districts, and even lawyers to be exhausting and ultimately unproductive. Curricula that can be managed more easily at home online can seem like a more productive, less time-consuming, and positive option.

But even if parents are not engaged in homeschooling, as most U.S. schools shift to one-to-one or high-access computing over the next few years every family will have at least one link to the worldwide web of learning and access to a giant library of e-books. Parents will have expanded access to English language acquisition and full translation services. Mobile learning applications will extend learning for the whole family. Students aren't the only ones who will be learning more; as they bring their own learning into the home, parents will have the opportunity to be involved in new ways, learning more themselves. The more they can go beyond monitoring to educating themselves about how to find ways to help their children learn, the better. Will the Internet make us smarter? It's a big net advantage but it is up to each of us to determine the extent to which digital learning will benefit our families.

PREDICTIONS

In five years . . .

Those learning at home through homeschooling and virtual charter schools will double to six million students, or about 10 percent of all students.

The world of digital learning is creating new roles for parent activists and advocates. Although vastly outspent, parents seeking educational alternatives have always proved to be a potent foe for the status quo. Groups such as Parent Revolution, which seeks to empower "parents to transform their own children's low-performing schools through community organizing," rely on a website, social networking, messaging, e-mail, and shoe leather to connect with parents and mobilize them on demand.[1] This power will be even more potent in an environment in which parents can take on the role of entrepreneur themselves and start up schools and programs powered by the Internet.

Rose Fernandez is one such involved parent. She is mother to five children, three at home and enrolled in a virtual charter school. Rose directs the National Parent Network for Online Learning and was the leading parent voice during a successful but contentious 2008 battle to change Wisconsin state law to protect online schools. Rose is a former trauma nurse and hospital administrator who now works nationally to increase awareness of the value of online education and encourage other parents to share how it serves their families.

TEACHING OUTSIDE THE BOX

Here's how you currently become a teacher. First, you decide on whether you want to teach secondary school or elementary. If K–8, you sit through a degree's worth of coursework full of education theory, do some student teaching, and get a certificate. For a high school certificate, in most states, you study a specific subject area—English, Spanish, math, history, or biology, for example—after which you spend a year getting your single subject teaching credential. If you don't get a credential, you can't teach at a public school. You could have a PhD in a subject. Like me, you could have taught MBA students for most of a decade. Like Sal Khan, you could be an exceptional tutor but you would not be allowed into the public schools. Private schools, yes. If you managed to make your way into a public school under an alternative certification you'd probably remain a liability because you do not help the school fulfill the requirement to have "highly qualified teachers" according to federal regulations.

This whole certification process doesn't seem to improve teacher effectiveness. It's an expensive barrier to entry that keeps talent out of schools. But Internet and learning entrepreneurs are changing that for teachers. They are creating a web of informal learning opportunities, free tools for teachers, and online schools. They are creating new opportunities for people interested in contributing to student learning.

Although public schools will always likely need some kind of credentialing system for vetting the teachers they hire, the opportunities for people to teach outside the box of the public school system are expanding. Take, for example, PhD student Gail Carmichael, who is studying computer science at Carleton University in Ottawa, Canada, and is passionate about using learning games to help girls develop and pursue interests in what are traditionally male-dominated areas such as engineering, science, and technology. Says Carmichael, "I like to help girls who might enjoy the topic see what it's really all about, and make it less scary for them to give it a try."[2] A decade ago, Gail probably would have become a teacher. She's studying a field that didn't exist a few years ago. Personal digital learning, serious games in particular, is expanding career options for people like Gail.

Digital learning has changed the world of learning outside of schools and so the world in which teachers can ply their trade, such as Kaplan and Sylvan, has developed sophisticated personalized learning systems. These companies are selling access to parents concerned about success in school. They offer great opportunities for learning professionals interested in part-time work, as well as flexible conditions.

Another example of innovations creating new, more flexible roles for teachers is the work of Carl Dorvil, who started Group Excellence (GE) in his Southern Methodist University dorm room. The son of Haitian

---

PREDICTIONS

In ten years . . .

There will be several do-it-yourself (DIY) high school options with an engaging merit badge sequence that will allow students to take ownership of and direct their own learning—with lots of teacher support, but when, where, and how students need it.

148

immigrants, Carl never took his education for granted. He was the first African American president of his high school and balanced four jobs while completing a triple major and starting a business as an undergraduate. Carl went on to finish an MBA in 2008. Today Group Excellence employs about four hundred people in four cities and serves over twenty thousand Texas students. Group Excellence provides tutoring services to struggling low-income students. Dorvil says, "The knowledge that I gained from business school propelled GE into becoming a respected tutoring company." Carl recruits talented college students to do much of the tutoring, but he's really looking for role models. "We don't believe we are a tutoring company that mentors, we believe we are a mentoring company that tutors and that has made all the difference." In one Dallas middle school, math scores shot up from 12 percent to more than 60 percent passing the state test only eight months after activating the Group Excellence program.[3] Carl Dorvil is a great example of a young entrepreneur contributing to student learning.

A NEW BOX CALLED TEACHING

Although personal digital learning is offering new opportunities for people who might otherwise have been teachers, it is also fundamentally changing the job of those who are teaching in our public schools. The job of teaching is going to start looking very different. As Diane Laufenberg, whose TED talk I discussed in Chapter Five, points out, the easy access we now have to information has changed the roles of schools and teachers. She challenges teachers to rethink what learning can look like in "a landscape where we let go of the idea that kids have come to school to get the information." Instead, she says, we need to ask them, challenge them, and help them find a way to figure out not just how to get the information but what they are going to do with it.[4]

In this new landscape of personal digital learning teachers are going to have to fire themselves once and for all from the job of expert and fully embrace the new job of facilitator, guide, and organizer. If you teach for a school district now, by 2013 you should expect to work in a school system that is based on the following premises:

1. Students have full-time access to mobile learning technology.

2. Students have access to comprehensive online instructional materials.

3. Student learning is accurately gauged by online assessments.

4. Students advance based on demonstrated competence.

5. Students are ready for your class and lesson.

6. You should not have to teach a course you're not equipped to teach.

7. You should be able to connect with other teachers facing similar challenges.

8. You should be able to support your learning with online tools and experiences.

9. You should be recognized for your contribution.

10. You should be allowed to add responsibility (and compensation) as you demonstrate results.

As the work of teachers changes and as the boundaries between home and school start to blur, students become the focal point for learning. It is happening with each student in its own unique way. Personal digital learning is changing the job of being a student.

TEACHING ONLINE

As we saw in Chapter Six, the world of virtual schools is creating new kinds of jobs for teachers, offering a level of engagement with individual students and flexibility not available to classroom teachers. Lindsay Woods is a K–6 teacher and part-time learning coach for some subjects for her first-grade son, who is a student in an online, virtual school. She is able to juggle it all during a typical week with a little time-shifting that sometimes includes evening history and weekend science for her son. According to Lindsay, "Shifting to teaching online was like being a new teacher all over again," but after a few years she loves the flexibility and time at home with her son. Lindsay credits her husband for supporting her learning coach role as well.[5]

Like all educators at virtual schools, Lindsay works out of a home office with a K^{12}-provided laptop that occasionally goes on the road with her. About half of her time is prescheduled with calls, synchronous instruction, class meetings, and other online meetings; the other half is tutoring, coaching, grading work, and trouble-shooting. Although some teachers may worry that working out of a home office is isolating, Nancy Brosnahan, academic administrator for the Virginia Virtual Academy, appreciates the amount of collaboration among online teachers. Rather than being isolated, Nancy and her colleagues think of teaching online as a team sport and actively take advantages of mutual strengths.

THE NEW JOB OF STUDENT

It's not that all students must become experts in every subject they are learning about—although specific areas of expertise can more easily emerge and be pursued as students are given more access, freedom, and encouragement—but students will need to become experts in another, more important area: their own learning. New technology will help them manage their own learning and develop a better feel for how they learn best, and give them the freedom to customize their own learning paths.

This greater self-awareness and freedom brings with it new responsibilities and opportunities for students to better advocate for themselves. This doesn't mean that parents or teachers give up this role altogether but they become partners in helping students become better advocates. Most students are supreme networkers. They use social networking sites in sophisticated ways but new digital learning environments will challenge students to create and participate in networks that drive learning and involvement. They will do more peer tutoring, they will make broader applications of their learning by connecting with experts, and they will put their learning to work through community service.

ADMINISTRATE THIS

The old job of principals, or, as they were called, "building managers," was to ensure compliance with local, state, and federal programs. Accountability shifted the focus to student learning. The "new normal" of the fiscal crisis introduced productivity: how to do more for less. Now many school leaders are laser focused on learning, struggling with tight budgets, and looking for ways to use technology to boost achievement. As a former private equity investor, for example, Rocketship Education CEO John Danner spent time thinking about return on investment. Now he's applying that sort of productivity-seeking instinct to elementary schools. As profiled in

Chapter Six, Rocketship uses learning technology to stretch the day, the year, and the budget. There is an intentional shift of instructional responsibility for a portion of the student day to an online environment to boost learning and reduce operating costs.

State and district leaders have the historic opportunity and grand challenge to lead through the pivot to personal digital learning. The fundamental rules of education are shifting and the change process is complicated in its academic, fiscal, political, and human dimensions. During this decade most U.S. schools will adopt models that blend online learning and on-site support, which means most U.S. superintendents and principals will manage through what former North Carolina Virtual Public School CEO Bryan Setser called "a perfect storm of reform." His advice includes the following: abandon seat-time requirements (get a waiver if you have to), stop buying textbooks, use open education resources on inexpensive tablet computers, and stretch staffing by moving students online for at least part of the day.[6] While facilitating changes like this, leaders will need to host ongoing community conversations, model professional learning, and demonstrate project management and resilience.

This will be an exciting but very challenging decade. The list of tools and potential partners available to schools grows every month. A decade of steady growth in educational entrepreneurship funded by foundations is now red hot with venture and private equity funding. It's all expanding the ways that learning professionals can contribute to student learning.

EDUPRENEURS

Fred Wilson, a managing partner at Union Square Ventures, said, "There is a general consensus that web startups are being created at a faster rate than ever."[7] That is certainly the case in the learning space; by 2010, there were double the number of start-ups every month compared to 2008. The ability to rapidly and inexpensively create web applications, the promise of viral business models, and the interest of investors have increased the number of learning start-ups, which is creating a new kind of edupreneur. Since about 2000, we've seen an explosion of school developers, managed school networks, school improvement providers, and advocacy organizations, all funded by new-money foundations. Teach For America helped to make education cool as a career by marketing a two-year service commitment to selective college graduates and, in lower numbers, career changers. TFA has recruited more than twenty thousand very bright people into education since Wendy Kopp's senior proposal at Princeton in 1990; some remain teachers, some become principals, others finish their commitment and start nonprofits, run foundations, or seek elected office—the alumni are a powerful force for social good.

There used to be one job in learning—teacher—with one salary schedule and benefits focused on retirement. The rise of the edupreneur is expanding the number of roles for learning professionals and these nontraditional learning roles are doubling every two or three years with an expanding array of options and employers. Nic Borg, an edupreneur in his own right, is enthusiastic about the potential for entrepreneurs. He was the technology director in a small suburban school district where, a few years earlier, he had been a high school senior. A year later, Nic was president of the largest and fastest-growing social learning platform in education. Working weekends and evenings with his partner Jeff O'Hara, Nic wrote the initial code for Edmodo in 2008. "We saw teachers trying to leverage social networks and social media to improve learning in their classrooms but struggling because those sites are blocked and not designed for classroom communications."

The opportunities are rapidly expanding. "The number of new startups in this area," notes Nic, "has exploded over the past few years, and has created a climate ripe for innovation. These tools are rapidly displacing the previous generation of learning management systems, and take advantage of a new wave of gadgets, and the increased fluency in social media of both students and teachers."[8]

MAKING A DIFFERENCE

"Life is difficult." I read the first line in *The Road Less Traveled* on my first day off after my first year as a superintendent and thought to myself, "M. Scott Peck should try being a school superintendent." Peck describes love as "extending yourself to benefit another."[9] At that point, I turned the book sideways and wrote "teaching" in big letters in the margin. Helping another person learn is the greatest gift a person can give. Becoming a school teacher is still the best way to give the gift of learning, but there is an expanding array of learning professions in which skill and passion can unite to make a difference. Similar to doctors, lawyers, and accountants, learning professionals finally have the opportunity to freelance, start a business, build a nonprofit, or join a public system.

Jay Kimmelman is a serial edupreneur but he is also an educator. After graduating from Harvard in 1999, Jay founded Edusoft to bring simple scanning technology to education assessment at a time when nearly every state was planning to implement standards and assessments. By 2003, Edusoft had achieved revenues of $20 million and Jay sold the company to Houghton Mifflin. That launched a worldwide journey to study the obstacles faced by people living in poverty. Jay spent eighteen months studying subsistence farming in a remote Chinese village. In 2007, Jay moved to Kenya and launched Bridge International Academies, an affordable network of schools serving families in the slums of Nairobi for about $50 per year. Jay built a scalable "school in a box" model by relentlessly driving down the cost of each component and pushing up the quality. Jay was not trained as an educator but may do more to improve access to quality education in Africa than anyone in history.

Jay is just one of thousands of new educators inventing the future by building new tools and new schools. Edupreneurs such as Jay will do as much to shape life on this planet as their counterparts in biotech, clean tech, or agri tech.

CONCLUSION

Getting Smart

Rick Hess and Olivia Meeks concluded *Customized Schooling* by suggesting the following:

> The one-size-fits-all school system has passed its expiration date. It is not that there was something innately wrong with the "one best system" or the conventional schoolhouse. Indeed, they represented the best practice solutions of an earlier, more bureaucratic era. Today, however, heightened aspirations, the press of student needs, and the opportunities presented by new tools and technologies mean that old arrangements are no longer a good fit. The charge is for schooling to make the same shift from the centralized, industrial model to a more nimble, customized model that we have made in so many other areas of life.[1]

The learning revolution under way is the shift from print to digital, lectures to interaction, testing to instant feedback, classes to individuals, schools to anywhere. The revolution will yield powerful learning platforms of customized playlists of engaging learning media, integrated team-based projects that leverage social media and community assets, and tailored student support services. The revolution will yield a new generation of schools that blend modes, extend learning, and incorporate community resources.

This country changes in fits and starts, especially in education, where barriers slow innovation diffusion. I travel every week to visit schools, educators, investors, policy makers, and entrepreneurs. Some days it's like being transported back fifty years and other days it feels like visiting the future. The learning revolution is under way but progress will be lumpy and dependent on leaders who make children a priority. The full potential of the digital future becomes widely available when money follows the student to the best learning experience, when students aren't bound by time and place, when they have access to the best teachers regardless of location, and after we solve a few privacy and security issues. Students will win when public education values inventiveness over tradition, responsiveness over hierarchy, and collaboration over exclusivity.

BENDING THE CURVE

KIPP, a network of charter schools, has produced strong academic results by doubling productive time on task for kids who need it most through a combination of a long day and year and double blocks of time focused on basic skills. It would be hard to replicate this full court press everywhere because it's expensive and relies on heroic effort. But now, for the first time in history, we have a chance to bend the learning curve. Technology has driven productivity and service breakthroughs in every other sector—education is next. The premise of this book is that we can do even better than KIPP. By providing 24/7 access to learning (Chapter Five) and by increasing engagement (Chapter Four) we can cost-effectively double productive time on task for kids who need it most. By customizing learning—teaching the best way at the right level (Chapter Three)—we can make each hour of learning more productive.

The combination of these factors, ignited by increased private and philanthropic investment, will improve achievement and completion rates in the United States. In emerging economies, hundreds of millions of young people will leapfrog traditional models of schooling and will gain access to quality school-as-a-service with very low-cost mobile technology.

Spend twenty minutes studying KnowledgeWorks' map of the future (www.futureofed.org/). You'll recognize that most of the "predictions" are already occurring; they just haven't had any noticeable effect on schooling. What's more jarring than the map is the introduction:

> If you think our future will require better schools, you're wrong. The future of education calls for entirely new kinds of learning environments.
>
> If you think we will need better teachers, you're wrong. Tomorrow's learners will need guides who take on fundamentally different roles.
>
> As every dimension of our world evolves so rapidly, the education challenges of tomorrow will require solutions that go far beyond today's answers.[2]

The revolution is on. The shift is inevitable but it will vary in form and time depending on local leadership and the extent to which communities put children and learning first. The status quo has massive gravity but is being enveloped by a new digital learning ecosystem. Edupreneurs have big new levers to shape the learning landscape—powerful apps, cheap devices, expanding broadband, and hundreds of millions of people ready to get smart.

Personal digital learning will change the world. Right in front of us is the opportunity to build new tools and schools that will help young people around the world learn more, faster, deeper, and cheaper. New tools will boost engagement and persistence. New schools will reach and lift kids from Detroit to Delhi, Newark to Nairobi. Hundreds of millions of young people will connect with college and careers. That may not be world peace but it's heading in the right direction.

APPENDIX
Getting Smart Toolkit

Reports About the Future of Learning

What You Can Do to Accelerate Learning

Ten Elements of High-Quality Digital Learning for State Policy Makers

Building Your Blended Learning School

List of Websites of Key Organizations

REPORTS ABOUT THE FUTURE OF LEARNING

If you want to learn more about the future of learning, here's a list of the ten most important reports for you to read.

1. *The Rise of K–12 Blended Learning* (Innosight Institute; Michael B. Horn and Heather Staker; January 2011)

   www.innosightinstitute.org/innosight/wp-content/uploads/ 2011/01/The-Rise-of-K-12-Blended-Learning.pdf

2. *Keeping Pace with K–12 Online Learning* (Evergreen Education Group; John Watson, Amy Murin, Lauren Vashaw, Butch Gemin, Chris Rapp, et al.; November 2010)

   www.kpk12.com/wp-content/uploads/KeepingPaceK12_ 2010.pdf

3. *A National Primer on K-12 Online Learning, Version 2* (iNACOL; Matthew Wicks; October 2010)

   www.inacol.org/research/docs/iNCL_NationalPrimerv 22010-web.pdf

4. *Blended Learning: The Convergence of Online and Face-to-Face Education* (NACOL; John Watson; 2008)

   www.inacol.org/research/promisingpractices/NACOL_ PP-BlendedLearning-lr.pdf

5. *Clearing the Path: Creating Innovation Space for Serving Over-Age, Under-Credited Students in Competency-Based Pathways.* (iNACOL; Chris Sturgis, Bob Rath, Ephraim Weisstein, and Susan Patrick; January 2011)

   www.inacol.org/research/docs/ClearingthePathReportJan 2011.pdf

6. *When Success Is the Only Option: Designing Competency-Based Pathways for Next Generation Learning* (iNACOL; Chris Sturgis and Susan Patrick; November 2010)

   www.inacol.org/research/competency/docs/iNACOL_SuccessOnlyOptn_Report011111-lr.pdf

7. *Transforming American Education: Learning Powered by Technology. National Education Technology Plan 2010* (U.S. Department of Education; 2010)

   www.ed.gov/sites/default/files/netp2010.pdf

8. *The Online Learning Imperative: A Solution to Three Looming Crises in Education* (Alliance for Excellent Education; Bob Wise with Robert Rothman; June 2010)

   www.all4ed.org/files/OnlineLearning.pdf

9. *Game Changer: Investing in Digital Play to Advance Children's Learning and Health* (The Joan Ganz Cooney Center at Sesame Workshop; Ann My Thai, David Lowenstein, Dixie Ching, and David Rejeski; June 2009)

   www.joanganzcooneycenter.org/upload_kits/game_changer_final_1.pdf

10. *Opportunity at the Top: How America's Best Teachers Could Close the Gaps, Raise the Bar, and Keep Our Nation Great* (Public Impact; Bryan C. Hassel and Emily Ayscue Hassel; 2010)

    http://opportunityculture.org/images/stories/opportunity_report_web.pdf

WHAT YOU CAN DO TO ACCELERATE LEARNING

The following pages include five or ten things that students, parents, teachers, principals, community members, policy makers, and edupreneurs can do to accelerate learning.

HIGH SCHOOL STUDENTS

1. Don't waste time; there are two hundred million kids working harder than you.

2. Take more math and find your own way to learn. Try tutorials like Khan Academy and games like those found on Mangahigh.

3. Pick a path: fast or selective. If fast, you can graduate from high school in three years with college credit if you plan ahead and take an online summer community college course or two.

4. If you want to go to a selective university, stick around for four years and take a handful of online Advanced Placement, International Baccalaureate, or dual-enrollment courses.

5. Build your resume and portfolio with examples of writing, problem solving, career exposure, and community service (and don't be an unemployable Facebook idiot).

PARENTS, GUARDIANS, AND FAMILIES

1. Build your own online learning plan. Pick a learning topic each year and build a podcast library to watch when you have a few extra minutes. Make sure your kids see you learning. Talk about what you're learning.

2. Be intentional about dinnertime conversations, field trips, and summer projects.

3. Manage student time online; a little recreation is great but they have work to do and it's your job to see that they do it.

4. Tell your eighth-graders that they'll be doing college work in two years and help them make a high school choice that facilitates Advanced Placement, International Baccalaureate, and or dual-enrollment credit.

5. Figure out your children's motivational profile. What interests spark curiosity? What activities promote persistence? Help them find ways to do more of what works for them in and out of school.

TEACHERS

1. Build a great iGoogle blogroll and spend at least fifteen minutes every day learning about learning.

2. Become an expert in teaching with technology. There are dozens of blogs worth reading. Start with Lisa Nielsen's *Innovative Educator* (http://theinnovativeeducator.blog spot.com/). Jason T. Bedell has a comprehensive online guide to teaching with technology (or buy the book).[1]

3. Join an online content group on Edmodo and share great material and strategies.

4. Attend an iNACOL weekly webinar.

5. Enlist student help in tech support at school. Encourage students to be tech contributors in their community.

6. Build a learning game and simulation playlist for your students to extend learning through weekends, breaks, and

summer vacation. Find one at http://MyHomeLearning .com.

7. Use cell phones, text messages, and voice mail to build the home-school bridge.

8. Lead a professional development session online; teach a class online.

9. Tell your principal or superintendent that you want to start a blended school.

10. Start a blog (or contribute to www.GettingSmart.com).

SCHOOL LEADERS

1. Visit an online school and a blended school.

2. Attend an iNACOL leadership webinar.

3. Start a community conversation with guest speakers and virtual field trips.

4. Extend learning with smart phones and tablets.

5. Build parent partnerships with social networking, text messaging, and voice mail.

6. Make reading a family affair with opportunities to learn at home and at school.

7. Create a working group to develop a blended learning plan.

8. Develop a transition budget with a grant, a business partner, or a year-end surplus.

9. Start the new year with digital content and one-to-one access (or a high-access environment).

10. Join a learning group on Edutopia, on LinkedIn, or in your district.

COMMUNITY MEMBERS AND BUSINESS PARTNERS

1. Lead a community field trip to visit an online and a blended school.

2. Host community conversations about workforce requirements, educational options, and the shift to personal digital learning.

3. Mentor and tutor students who need extra help.

4. Provide relevant opportunities including internships and projects.

5. Help sponsor the transition to personal digital learning with a donation, assistance with project planning, or training.

LEARNING PROFESSIONALS

1. Focus your learning: know as much as anyone about your job—understand the context, master the tasks, and improve the work products.

2. Broaden your learning: pick a new topic each year and go deep, connect your deep dives to career objectives and interests, find out what smart people are reading and learning.

3. Manage your learning: think about your learning like a project and manage it—set some goals, track it, look for ways to learn more faster.

4. Reflect on your learning: journal or blog about your learning—you'll never really know what you know until you write it down.

5. Portfolio your learning. Use LinkedIn and Facebook as your portfolio—catalog your work product, ask for references.

SCHOOL BOARD MEMBERS AND LEGISLATORS

1. Read *Digital Learning Now!* (summary in the next section).[2]

2. Check out your state's progress in *Keeping Pace 2010* (www.kpk12.com).

3. Hold a hearing and community meeting about digital learning.

4. Build support for rewriting district policy or state education code.

5. Introduce a policy or bill to expand statewide online and dual-enrollment opportunities.

CORPORATE EXECUTIVES

1. Make learning a priority for your employees.

2. Let your employees make family learning a priority; give them flexibility to be involved in their children's education.

3. Use your position to advance personal digital learning opportunities in your community and state.

EDUPRENEURS

1. Read GettingSmart (www.GettingSmart.com/) and AVC (www.avc.com/) daily, EdNET Insight News Alerts (www.ednetinsight.com/news-alerts) weekly, and neXtup (www.nextupresearch.com/Site/neXtup.html) reports periodically.

2. Build an idea pipeline and rate opportunities by market size, competition, and barriers to entry. Pick the most attractive one that you are most passionate about—something you can spend eighteen hours a day working on for years.

3. Determine the best source of capital for your idea. A nonprofit organization can be a good option if you are more interested in meeting a need than scaling and if you think you can find grants to kickstart it. Fueling a for-profit venture with private capital may be even harder, but good ideas attract capital. Bootstrap as much as you can with friends and family funding.

4. Build your team carefully; make changes quickly.

5. Understand everything about your customer's world.

6. Keep the burn low, stay virtual, use grants and contracts to get smart and build capacity. Sell every day.

7. If you can afford to, give away a core feature, let it grow virally, use customer feedback to make improvements, wait to turn on revenue streams until you've gained some traction.

8. Use social media to extend your reach and build some buzz. Ask your customers to blog for you.

9. Find a mentor, start a personal learning network, and learn everything you can from the start-up failures of others.

TEN ELEMENTS OF HIGH-QUALITY DIGITAL LEARNING FOR STATE POLICY MAKERS

Former governors Jeb Bush and Bob Wise recognized the potential of and barriers to personal digital learning. They knew that state leadership including the governor, legislature, and state education agency would play a critical role in reform. They recruited almost one hundred experts and in about one hundred days developed recommendations for state leaders published in a report titled *Digital Learning Now!*[3] The ten elements are reprinted below with permission of the project sponsor, the Foundation for Excellence in Education.

1. *Student eligibility:* All students are digital learners.
   - State ensures access to high-quality digital content and online courses to all students (most states limit student access to courses offered at local schools).
   - State ensures access to high-quality digital content and online courses to students in K–12 at any time in their academic career (addresses restrictions placed on students previously educated at home or in private schools).

2. *Student access:* All students have access to high-quality digital content and online courses.
   - State does not restrict access to high-quality digital content and online courses with policies such as class size ratios and caps on enrollment or budget.
   - State does not restrict access to high-quality digital content and online courses based on geography, such as school district, county, or state.

- State requires students take high-quality online college- or career-prep courses to earn a high school diploma.

3. *Personalized learning:* All students can customize their education using digital content through an approved provider.
    - State allows students to take online classes full-time, part-time, or by individual course.
    - State allows students to enroll with multiple providers and blend online courses with on-site learning.
    - State allows rolling enrollment year round.
    - State does not limit the number of credits earned online.
    - State does not limit provider options for delivering instruction.

4. *Advancement:* Students progress based on demonstrated competency.
    - State requires matriculation based on demonstrated competency.
    - State does not have a seat-time requirement for matriculation.
    - State provides assessments when students are ready to complete the course or unit.

5. *Content:* Digital content, instructional materials, and online and blended learning courses are high quality.
    - State requires digital content and online and blended learning courses to be aligned with state standards or Common Core State Standards when applicable.

6. *Instruction:* Digital instruction and teachers are high quality.
    - State provides alternative certification routes, including online instruction and performance-based certification.

- State provides certification reciprocity for online instructors certified by another state.
- State creates the opportunity for multilocation instruction.
- State encourages postsecondary institutions with teacher-preparation programs to offer targeted digital instruction training.
- State ensures that teachers have professional development or training to better use technology and before teaching an online or blended learning course.

7. *Providers:* All students have access to multiple high-quality providers.
    - State has an open, transparent, and expeditious approval process for digital learning providers.
    - State provides students with access to multiple approved providers including public, private, and nonprofit.
    - State treats all approved education providers—public, chartered, and private—equally.
    - State provides all students with access to all approved providers.
    - State has no administrative requirements that would unnecessarily limit participation of high-quality providers (e.g., office location).
    - State provides easy-to-understand information about digital learning, including programs, content, courses, tutors, and other digital resources, to students.

8. *Assessment and accountability:* Student learning is the metric for evaluating the quality of content and instruction.
    - State administers assessments digitally.
    - State ensures a digital formative assessment system.

- State evaluates the quality of content and courses predominately based on student learning data.
- State evaluates the effectiveness of teachers based, in part, on student learning data.
- State holds schools and providers accountable for achievement and growth.

9. *Funding:* Funding creates incentives for performance, options, and innovation.
    - State funding model pays providers in installments that incentivize completion and achievement.
    - State allows for digital content to be acquired through instructional material budgets and does not discourage digital content with print adoption practices.
    - State funding allows customization of education including choice of providers.

10. *Delivery:* Infrastructure supports digital learning.
    - State is replacing textbooks with digital content, including interactive and adaptive multimedia.
    - State ensures high-speed broadband Internet access for public school teachers and students.
    - State ensures all public school students and teachers have Internet access devices.
    - State uses purchasing power to negotiate lower-cost licenses and contracts for digital content and online courses.
    - State ensures local and state data systems and related applications are updated and robust to inform longitudinal management decisions, accountability, and instruction.

BUILDING YOUR BLENDED LEARNING SCHOOL

The answers to these thirteen questions will help you develop a school model that productively blends online and onsite learning.

1. Who will attend?
   - Define grade levels and the geographic service area. Where will students come from? Where will they continue their education?
   - What college awareness partnerships and dual-enrollment opportunities can be created?
   - What community assets can be leveraged (e.g., museums, youth and family services)?

2. What should students know and be able to do?
   - Build an intellectual mission robust enough to design a school around, one that incorporates a view of human development and citizenship.
   - Build on state standards or Common Core State Standards but frame academic aspirations with clarity and a sense of priority.
   - What emerging industry clusters are likely to be the basis of growth in family wage employment regionally?

3. In what ways will students learn?
   - A core curriculum of online courses is easy to administer and support but first-generation content is flat and sequential; they are better than textbooks in that rate, time, and place become variable.
   - Engaging and adaptive next-generation learning experiences are becoming more plentiful but not yet easy to glue together into coherent pathways. If you

decide to ditch the first-generation courseware and go with components, make sure you have teachers who can pull it off.

- Integrated projects are a great way to extend and apply an online core curriculum but make sure they are standards-aligned and rigorously assessed.

4. How will they show what they know?
   - Take advantage of online adaptive, formative, and content-embedded assessment.
   - Require students to show what they know in regular demonstrations of learning.
   - A mixed assessment model provides rich information about each student but is likely to require a customized dashboard—another benefit of participating in a network of schools.

5. How will students progress?
   - Students should have the ability to move at their own pace and get extra help when they need it, particularly in math.
   - Take advantage of cohort benefits with seminar dialogs, project teams, study groups, social learning groups, and peer tutoring.

6. What role will teachers play?
   - The courseware or components adopted should allow students to learn semiautonomously for at least a portion of the day, allowing larger staffing ratios than typical. Some online activities can be supervised by noncertificated staff. The combination of more autonomous work and alternative supervision creates time for master teachers to teach small groups of students and to mentor junior staff.

- Some subjects, possibly including advanced courses, foreign languages, and some special needs instruction, may be taught best by teachers working remotely.

7. What role will students play?
    - Digital learning enables more self-directed learning, especially in middle and high school. Giving students some choices about what academic challenges to attack and in what ways they will demonstrate competency can create more ownership.
    - Digital learning can be used to extend the day and the year, and, for some students, can double time spent on core skill development.
    - Create opportunities for student voice in the life of the school.
    - Peer tutoring is a great way to extend and apply learning.

8. How will student learning be supported?
    - An online core curriculum can be supported by 24/7 online tutoring to provide just-in-time support.
    - Middle and high school students should be supported by online guidance to promote college and career awareness and support appropriate course selection.
    - Students need active links to community-based youth and family services.

9. How will students access learning?
    - Tablets look like a good option for student access devices but a full keyboard netbook will still be better at supporting a substantial amount of daily writing.
    - Broadband at home facilitates extended learning. For those without, it may be possible to identify community access strategies or content that does not require Internet access.

10. How much time will students spend at school?
    - Like Rocketship, blended models can extend the day by 25 percent with little additional cost.
    - A regional school could host two shifts of students that attend two or three days per week.
    - A mostly virtual school can offer a one-day-per-week check-in for guidance and tutoring.

11. What is the learning calendar?
    - A quarter system provides three breaks of at least two weeks that can be used to extend and enrich learning opportunities. If stretched out over 240 days and combined with extended-day options the quarter system could double core academic time for some students.

12. What is the opening or transition budget?
    - A generous tradition is to have a principal on board for a planning year. It's a good idea to have a core team together for at least six months to finalize plans, begin building culture, and coordinate an effective hiring process.
    - A generous preopening budget is $1.5 million for planning, marketing, and hiring, excluding opening losses, deposits, and furniture, fixtures, and equipment.

13. Is the model sustainable and scalable?
    - At or before full enrollment, the model should break even (and not require philanthropic support).
    - More efficient school models can generate sufficient operating surplus to partially fund the growth of a network.

LIST OF WEBSITES OF KEY ORGANIZATIONS

Academic Earth, www.academicearth.org

AdvancePath Academics, www.advancepath.com/ (a Learn Capital portfolio company)

American Indian Foundation, www.aifoundation.org/

American Institutes for Research, www.air.org/

Apex Learning, http://apexlearning.com/

Aptech, www.aptech-worldwide.com

Association for High School Innovation, www.ahsi.org/

AUSL, www.ausl-chicago.org/

AVC, www.AVC.com

Big Picture Learning, www.bigpicture.org/

Bridge International Academies, www.bridgeinternational academies.com/Bridge/Home.html (a Learn Capital portfolio company)

The Bridgespan Group, www.bridgespan.org/

BrightStorm, www.brightstorm.com/

Campaign for the Civic Mission of Schools, http://civicmission ofschools.org

Career Launcher, www.CareerLauncher.com

Center for Civic Education, http://new.civiced.org/

Charter School Growth Fund, www.chartergrowthfund.org/

Charter Schools USA, www.charterschoolsusa.com/

City Light Capital, www.citylightcap.com

CK-12, www.ck12.org/flexbook/

Colorado Children's Campaign, www.coloradokids.org/

Common Core State Standards Initiative, www.corestandards .org/

Communities In Schools, www.cisga.org/plc/plc_whatare.php

Connections Academy, www.connectionsacademy.com

Cramster, www.Cramster.com

Curriki, www.curriki.org/

Dasra, www.dasra.org

Designmate, www.designmate.com/

Digital Learning Now!, www.digitallearningnow.com/

DreamBox Learning, www.dreambox.com/

Early College High School Initiative, www.earlycolleges.org/

Edmodo, www.edmodo.com/ (a Learn Capital portfolio company)

EdNet Alerts, www.ednetinsight.com/news-alerts

The Education Arcade, www.educationarcade.org/

Educomp Solutions, www.Educomp.com (a Revolution portfolio company)

Edvisions Schools, www.edvisionsschools.org/custom/Splash Page.asp

Empathy Learning Systems, http://enterprisingschools.com/ aps-networks/service-providers/training-institute/empathy-learning-systems

Envictus, www.envictus.com/

ETS, www.ets.org/

Evoke, www.urgentevoke.com/

Fabindia, www.fabindia.com/

Flat World Knowledge, www.flatworldknowledge.com/

Getting Smart, www.GettingSmart.com/

GoingOn, www.goingon.com/

Gray Matters Capital, www.graymatterscapital.com

GreatSchools, www.greatschools.org/

Guaranteach, www.guaranteach.com/

Hooked On Phonics, www.hookedonphonics.com/

iCivics, www.icivics.org/

Indian School Finance Company, www.isfc.in

Innovations for Learning, www.innovationsforlearning.org/about_teachermate.php

The Innovative Educator, http://theinnovativeeducator.blogspot.com

Institute of Play, http://instituteofplay.org

International Association for K–12 Online Learning, www.iNACOL.org

IQity, www.iq-ity.com

Kaplan, www.kaplan.com/pages/default.aspx

Khan Academy, www.khanacademy.org/

KIPP, http://kipp.org/

Knewton, www.Knewton.com

KnowledgeWorks Foundation, http://knowledgeworks.org

KnowledgeWorks 2020 Forecast, http://knowledgeworks.org/action/our-work/creating-conditions-change/2020-forecast

Kunskapsskolan, www.kunskapsskolan.se (Swedish home: U.S. site is www.kunskapsskolan.com/sitescontact/usa.4.52155b18 128a87c7cfd80009919.html)

K^{12}, www.k12.com/

Lafafa Kids Education, www.lafafa.net/ (a Learn Capital portfolio company)

L.A.'s Promise, http://laspromise.org/

Learn Capital, www.LearnCapital.com

The Leona Group, L.L.C., www.leonagroup.com/

Lockheed Martin Virtual World Labs, www.lockheedmartin.com/data/assets/sts/ProductCards/VWLABS_pc.pdf

Mangahigh.com, www.mangahigh.com (a Learn Capital portfolio company)

McKinsey & Company, www.mckinsey.com/

Mosaica Education, http://mosaicaeducation.com/

My Home Learning, http://MyHomeLearning.com/

National Alliance of Concurrent Enrollment Partnerships, http://nacep.org/

National Heritage Academies, http://heritageacademies.com/

NBC Learn, http://archives.nbclearn.com/portal/site/k-12

NewGlobe Schools, www.newglobeschools.org/

NewSchools Venture Fund, www.newschools.org/

neXtup, www.nextupresearch.com/Site/neXtup.html

NYC iSchool, http://nycischool.org/

OER Commons, www.oercommons.org/

Open Education Solutions, http://openedsolutions.com/ (a Learn Capital portfolio company)

Open High School of Utah, www.openhighschool.org/

Parent Revolution, http://parentrevolution.org/

The Parthenon Group, www.parthenon.com/

The Partnership for 21st Century Skills, www.p21.org/

PBS Kids, www.PBSkids.org

PBS TeacherLine, www.pbs.org/teacherline/

Pearson, http://pearson.com/

P2PU, http://p2pu.org/

Quest to Learn, http://q2l.org/

Reasoning Mind, www.reasoningmind.org/

Re-Inventing Schools Coalition, www.reinventingschools.org/

Rocketship Education, http://rsed.org/

RosettaStone, www.rosettastone.com/

The Savvy Source, www.savvysource.com/

School of One, www.schoolofone.org/

SchoolTube, www.schooltube.com (a Learn Capital portfolio company)

StraighterLine, www.straighterline.com/

Strive for College Collaborative, www.striveforcollege.org/

Success for All Foundation, www.successforall.net/About/story.html

Sylvan Learning, http://tutoring.sylvanlearning.com/index.cfm

Teachers Pay Teachers, www.teacherspayteachers.com/

Teach For America, www.teachforamerica.org/

Teachscape, www.teachscape.com

TED, www.ted.com

Usha Martin, www.ushamartin.com/

VOISE Academy High, www.voise.cps.k12.il.us/

Western Governors University, www.wgu.edu

Wireless Generation, www.wirelessgeneration.com

WiZiQ, www.wiziq.com/

QUESTIONS AND ANSWERS

I talk about the learning revolution to a wide variety of audiences almost every week. Here are some of the questions I get:

- *How is this any different than radio and TV? Advocates said they would transform education and here we are.*

The web is interactive and ubiquitous. The curve-bending, adaptive potential of personalized learning is what really makes this different. It's the first chance in history to learn more, faster, and cheaper. Now that anyone can learn anything, anywhere that changes everything.

- *Is this just about making learning more fun and interesting?*

Higher levels of engagement will lead to more time on task and more learning per year. In the next decade, we'll become much more sophisticated about motivation and should be able to tailor learning sequences by learning level, interests, and motivational profile. When you combine engagement with 24/7 access to digital learning, it's an affordable way to double time on task for many students. Simulations and 3D animations will prove to be a much more powerful way to teach many aspects of science, calculus, and social systems. And finally, online learning allows us to rethink school architecture and staffing. Differentiated (different levels) and distributed (different locations) staffing leverages great teachers wherever they are. Together, the benefits of personal digital learning will help students learn more faster and help schools become more efficient.

- *People with access may be able to learn facts but not persistence, judgment, and wisdom.*

That may be true of Internet searching, but we're moving up the knowledge food chain. Learning games teach persistence. Social learning communities promote dialog. Virtual environments and simulations teach critical thinking. The question implies a fully automated learning system but for the foreseeable future virtual and blended learning environments will rely on powerful sustained learning relationships—and in many cases, those interactions will be more frequent and meaningful than in traditional environments.

- *Won't this cost more money?*

Blended schools can cost less to operate because they can use differentiated and distributed staffing and higher student ratios for portions of the day. States and districts will need to make investments in high-access environments (that is, provisions to ensure that every student has an Internet access device) but the switch to digital content and assessment often saves enough money to more than offset the total cost of access devices. U.S. schools should plan on switching from print to digital for the 2012–13 school year in preparation for new online state assessments. The switch will require some planning and some changes to policies and budgeting practices—start now.

- *It sounds like there are transition costs.*

The shift from a print education model to personal digital learning is a complicated project with academic, human resource, technology, financial, as well as policy and political dimensions. To make the shift more doable and affordable, most schools will want to break the process up into bite-size chunks: a few grades each year, digital content one year, and competency-based progress the next. It would be helpful to have grants to pay for outside expertise, project management, buying (rather than leasing) tablets or netbooks, and training. Without grants, schools may need to postpone some purchases and save money for a year to internally fund the transition.

- *Will opening up online enrollment to previously home-educated and private school students cost states money?*

Concerns about increased enrollment are real but likely to be quite small, perhaps 1 percent increases in some states. Because online learning is often 10 to 15 percent less expensive (even more savings on a per-course basis), the cost of increased enrollments is likely to be offset by savings recouped by traditional students enrolling in online courses.

- *Will online learning just become another unfunded mandate from states to districts? Shouldn't states pay for online learning?*

Several dozen states initially paid for online courses provided by the state and held districts harmless. As the programs scaled, the double payment for students became unsustainable. North Carolina is the most recent example of a state that ended up "double-dipping" and required districts to pay for the online courses—a money-follows-the-student system. The complicated mixture of local, state, and federal funding makes a funding-follows-the-student recommendation a challenge. The opportunities afforded by digital learning are further rationales for states to create more equitable funding systems that also encourage achievement and completion. Rather than being an unfunded mandate, online and blended learning is an opportunity for districts to simultaneously improve quality, expand options, and reduce cost.

- *Doesn't online and blended learning exacerbate the digital divide and achievement gap?*

Yes and no. New access devices and services always create a gap and may exacerbate parenting effects (good parents get even more effective at promoting learning) but technology will continue to get better and cheaper with wider access. As states and districts make provisions for one-to-one access, it will give every student twenty-four-hour access to quality learning opportunities. Technology may not close the achievement gap but it will close the preparation gap—more students will be adequately prepared for success in college and careers.

- *How will a playlist of experiences and a bunch of online courses add up to an education?*

Customized learning playlists have the potential to quickly build basic skills. A choice of online courses can ensure that every student has access to a comprehensive curriculum of consistent quality. But making sure that it adds up to a coherent education is still a challenge, maybe a bigger challenge. Worst-case scenario, it's an electronic version of the old shopping mall high school. Best-case scenario, blended schools will combine productive pathways of learning around a core intellectual mission and will encourage students to demonstrate important habits of mind.

- *What's the next big advance?*

Content embedded-assessment will be the most important development of the decade. Instead of weekly quizzes, students will soon receive dozens of forms of instant feedback daily from learning games, computer-scored writing, end-of-unit quizzes, simulations, and virtual environments. Once all this feedback is linked to the Common Core State Standards, the flood of achievement data will guide regular goal-setting conversations between a student and a teacher-advisor. The casual game space suggests that performance feedback can promote persistence, achievement, and self-directed progress.

- *How should teacher effectiveness be measured?*

Multiple measures should be used to make judgments about educator effectiveness. Obviously, we must include evidence that answers the question "are kids learning?" but the shift to personal digital learning is introducing new instructional experiences and new differentiated and distributed staffing models that make the "effectiveness" question more complicated. So build temporary agreements and update them every year or two.

- *Won't this all be superficial learning? Can computers promote deeper learning?*

I haven't factored a polynomial for a decade (and then it was to help my daughter with her homework) but I spend most of the day doing multivariable problem solving. Algebraic thinking is a keystone skill that every young person needs to engage in the idea economy and to be a contributing citizen. Systems thinking is a step beyond algebraic thinking with hundreds of equations and thousands of variables—and that's where there's real value added. Systems thinking is more about differential equations and rate of change than algebra. A good op-ed from David Brooks or Fareed Zakaria, an interview with investor Warren Buffet, or a game from Will Wright exhibits systems thinking and can influence your own mental model. Simulations and virtual environments (like good historical fiction) can teach facts as well as systems thinking—a potentially super-efficient way to build rich mental models. Schools that blend the best of online and on-site learning will combine well-constructed projects supported by targeted skill-building playlists. They will promote deeper learning. There are and will certainly be fast, cheap, and more superficial approaches to learning but the potential of personal digital learning is much greater.

- *What is the quality-control mechanism?*

With multiple statewide providers of online learning services, states play a critical role in contracting or chartering. Few states have sufficient capacity for this important performance contracting role; they should take a couple percent of funds off the top to fund oversight. In addition to a robust contracting function, states must enact the "good school promise" by closing and replacing persistently failing schools.

- *Will the new state assessments system help make the shift?*

The shift from paper to online tests will be a challenge for the states on many fronts including logistics, academics, politics, student access, bandwidth, and security. Race to the Top winners will be better able to resource transition plans. The shift from print to digital instructional materials will help pay for the transition but adds more complexity to the project.

The expansion of online and competency-based models adds another dimension of complexity to the design and implementation of online assessments. For example, end-of-course exams need to be available on demand (or frequently) to support individual progress. States and districts aren't ready for the flood of keystroke data that content-embedded assessments will produce.

It's time for states to build an integrated plan for the shift to personal digital learning starting with online testing. Online testing will produce better, cheaper, and faster performance feedback for students, teachers, and system heads. A four- to five-year-phased approach should start with surveys of computers and broadband (if not readily available) and a few pilots in September.

NOTES

FOREWORD

1. Wise, B., with Rothman, R. (2010, June). *The online learning imperative: A solution to three looming crises in education.* Alliance for Excellent Education. Retrieved from www.all4ed.org/files/OnlineLearning.pdf
2. Wise, 2010, June, ibid.
3. Christensen, C. M., Horn, M. B., & Johnson, C. W. (2008). *Disrupting class: How disruptive innovation will change the way the world learns.* New York: McGraw-Hill.

PREFACE

1. Bonk, C. J. (2009). *The world is open.* San Francisco: Jossey-Bass.

CHAPTER ONE: HOW PERSONAL DIGITAL LEARNING WILL MAKE US SMART

1. OECD. (2009, August 9). *Education at a glance: OECD indicators.* Retrieved from www.oecd.org/document/24/0,3343,en_2649_39263238_43586328_1_1_1_1,00.html
2. Gonzales, P., Williams, T., Jocelyn, L., Roey, S., Kastberg, D., & Brenwald, S. (2009, September). *Highlights from TIMSS 2007: Mathematics and science achievement of U.S. fourth- and eighth-grade students in an international context.* National Center for Education Statistics. Retrieved from http://nces.ed.gov/pubs2009/2009001.pdf
3. Anderson, N. (2010, November 18). Report: Nation's public schools are improving, but still have a long way to go. *Washington Post.*

Retrieved from www.washingtonpost.com/wp-dyn/content/article/ 2010/11/18/AR2010111802148.html?hpid=topnews

4. Autor, D. (2010, April). *The polarization of job opportunities in the U.S. labor market: Implications for employment and earnings.* Brookings Institution. Retrieved from www.brookings.edu/~/media/Files/ rc/papers/2010/04_jobs_autor/04_jobs_autor.pdf

5. Zakaria, F. (2010, October 21). Restoring the American dream. *Time Magazine.* Retrieved from www.time.com/time/nation/article/ 0,8599,2026776,00.html

6. Mayer, M. (2006, May 17). *Learning from mistakes.* [Video] Ecorner: Stanford University's Entrepreneurship Corner. Retrieved from http://ecorner.stanford.edu/authorMaterialInfo.html?mid=1528

7. Personal interview, June 25, 2010.

8. Vander Ark, T. (2010, May 2). *Toby Rowland, Mangahigh.* OpenEd Solutions. Retrieved from http://openedsolutions.com/toby-rowland-manga-high.html

9. Friedman, T. L. (2010, October 30). It's morning in India. *New York Times.* Retrieved from www.nytimes.com/2010/10/31/opinion/ 31friedman.html?_r=2&hp

10. Zakaria, 2010, October 21, op cit.

11. Schoeniger, G. (2010, June 21). *Entrepreneurs as insurgents.* E360 Blog. Retrieved from www.entrepreneurship.org/en/Blogs/e360-Blog/2010/June/Entrepreneurs-as-insurgents.aspx

12. Hess, F. M., & Manno, B. V., eds. (2011). *Customized schooling* (p. 193). Cambridge, MA: Harvard Education Press.

13. Adapted from Collins, A., & Halverson, R. (2009). *Rethinking education in the age of technology* (pp. 91–104). New York: Teachers College Press.

14. Neill, J. (2005, March 9). *Ten expeditionary learning principles.* Retrieved from http://wilderdom.com/experiential/tenELOBprinciples.html

CHAPTER TWO: AMERICAN EDUCATION

1. Tapscott, D. (2010, November 23). *New York Times* cover story on "Growing Up Digital" misses the mark. *Huffington Post.* Retrieved from www.huffingtonpost.com/don-tapscott/whats-wrong-with-the-new-_b_787819.html?page=3

2. Palfrey, J., & Gasser, U. (2008). *Born digital: Understanding the first generation of digital natives.* New York: Basic Books. Retrieved from www.borndigitalbook.com/excerpt.php

3. *New study shows time spent online important for teen development.* (2008, November 20). Digital Media & Learning Press Release. The John D. and Catherine T. MacArthur Foundation. Retrieved from www.macfound.org/site/c.lkLXJ8MQKrH/b.4773437/k.3CE6/New_Study_Shows_Time_Spent_Online_Important_for_Teen_Development.htm

4. Prensky, M. (2005, September). *Engage me or enrage me: What today's learners demand.* Retrieved from http://net.educause.edu/ir/library/pdf/erm0553.pdf

5. Association of American Colleges and Universities. (2010, November 15). *What is liberal education?* Retrieved from www.aacu.org/leap/what_is_liberal_education.cfm

6. Hirsch Jr., E. D. (2006). *The knowledge deficit: Closing the shocking education gap for American children.* New York: Houghton Mifflin.

7. KnowledgeWorks Foundation. (2010). *2020 forecast: Creating the future of learning.* Retrieved from www.futureofed.org/

8. Friedman, T. L. (2010, June 8). A gift for grads: Start-ups. *New York Times.* Retrieved from www.nytimes.com/2010/06/09/opinion/09friedman.html

9. Adapted from KnowledgeWorks Foundation, 2010, op cit.

CHAPTER THREE: CUSTOMIZATION

1. Patrick, S., & Sturgis, C. (2010, November 15). *When success is the only option: Designing competency-based pathways for next generation learning.* A Nellie Mae Education Foundation, MetisNet, and iNACOL report. Retrieved from www.inacol.org/research/competency/index.php

2. Vander Ark, T. (2011, January 6). *ASU & Knewton launch adaptive math pilot.* OpenEd Solutions. Retrieved from http://openedsolutions.com/asu-knewton-launch-adaptive-math-pilot.html

CHAPTER FOUR: MOTIVATION

1. Hawkins, R. (2010, August 20). *EVOKE reflections: Results from the World Bank's on-line education game (part 2).* EduTech. Retrieved from http://blogs.worldbank.org/edutech/evoke-reflections-results-from-the-world-banks-on-line-educational-game-part-2

2. McGonigal, J. (2010, March 10). *Gaming can make a better world.* [Video] TED Talks. Retrieved from www.ted.com/talks/lang/eng/jane_mcgonigal_gaming_can_make_a_better_world.html

3. Chatfield, T. (2010, November 15). *7 ways games reward the brain.* [Video] TED Talks. Retrieved from www.ted.com/talks/tom_ chatfield_7_ways_games_reward_the_brain.html

4. Chatfield, 2010, November 15, ibid.

5. Sinclair, M. (2011, February 22). Interactive game "Vanished" doubles as an educational tool. *USA Today.* Retrieved from www .usatoday.com/tech/gaming/2011–02–22-mystery22_ST_N.htm

6. Smithsonian Education. (2011, May). *Vanished.* Retrieved from www.smithsonianeducation.org/vanished/index.html

7. Pappas, Stephanie. (2011, March 14). Augmented reality game lets kids be the scientists. Retrieved from www.livescience.com/13211/ augmented-reality-game-lets-kids-scienists.html

8. Quest to Learn. (2011). *Reason and purpose.* Retrieved from http:// q2l.org/purpose

9. Corbett, S. (2010, September 19). Video games win a beachhead in the classroom. *New York Times.* Retrieved from www.nytimes .com/2010/09/19/magazine/19video-t.html?_r=2&pagewanted=2

10. Quest to Learn. (2011). *Key features.* Retrieved from http://q2l.org/ features

11. Thai, A. M., Lowenstein, D., Ching, D., & Rejeski, D. (2009). *Game changer: Investing in digital play to advance children's learning and health.* The Joan Ganz Cooney Center at Sesame Workshop. Retrieved from www.joanganzcooneycenter.org/Reports-18/.html

12. Trudeau, M. (2010, December 20). *Video games boost brain power, multitasking skills.* NPR. Retrieved from www.npr.org/2010/12/ 20/132077565/video-games-boost-brain-power-multitasking-skills

13. Vander Ark, T. (2010, November 10). *Richard Boyd, Lockheed.* OpenEd Solutions. Retrieved from http://openedsolutions.com/ richard-boyd-lockheed.html

CHAPTER FIVE: EQUALIZATION

1. Ted Conferences. (2010, November 15). TED. Retrieved from www. ted.com/index.php/pages/view/id/47

2. Laufenberg, D. (2010, November). *How to learn? From mistakes.* Retrieved from www.ted.com/talks/diana_laufenberg_3_ways_to_ teach.html

3. Hassel, B. C., & Hassel, E. A. (2010). *Opportunity at the top: How America's best teachers could close the gaps, raise the bar, and keep our*

nation great. Public Impact. Retrieved from www.publicimpact. com/component/content/article/67-opportunity-culture/255-opportunity-at-top

4. Vander Ark, T. (2009, February 2). *Private capital and public education: Toward quality at scale.* AEI Future of American Education Project. Working Paper 2009–02. American Enterprise Institute. Retrieved from www.aei.org/docLib/Vander%20Ark.pdf

5. Carter, M. (2010, November 8). A question of bridges. *National Journal.* Retrieved from http://education.nationaljournal.com/2010/ 11/a-question-of-bridges.php

6. Carter, 2010, November 8, ibid.

7. Strive for College. (2010, December 2). *Joseph Stiglitz speaks at Strive.* [Video] Retrieved from www.striveforcollege.org/media/video3.html

8. Vander Ark, T. (2010, June 4). *Presence Telecare: Online speech therapy.* OpenEd Solutions. Retrieved from http://openedsolutions.com/ presencetelecare-online-speech-therapy.html

9. Vander Ark, 2010, June 4, ibid.

CHAPTER SIX: INTEGRATION

1. Watson, J., Murin, A., Vashaw, L., Gemin, B., Rapp, C., et al. (2010). *Keeping pace with K–12 online learning: An annual review of policy and practice.* Evergreen Education. Retrieved from www.kpk12.com/ wp-content/uploads/KeepingPaceK12_2010.pdf

2. Christensen, C. M., Horn, M., & Johnson, C. W. (2008). *Disrupting class: How disruptive innovation will change the way the world learns.* New York: McGraw-Hill.

3. U.S. Department of Education. (2010, November 17). *The new normal: Doing more with less—Secretary Arne Duncan's remarks at the American Enterprise Institute.* Retrieved from www.ed.gov/news/ speeches/new-normal-doing-more-less-secretary-arne-duncans-remarks-american-enterprise-institut

4. Coates, T.-N. (2010, July–August). The little schoolhouse. *The Atlantic.* Retrieved from www.theatlantic.com/magazine/archive/2010/07/ the-littlest-schoolhouse/8132/

5. Dubner, S. J. (2010, May 12). *How is a bad radio station like the public school system?* [Blog comment] Freakonomics. Retrieved from www.freakonomics.com/2010/05/12/freakonomics-radio-how-is-a-bad-radio-station-like-the-public-school-system/

6. School of One. (2010, November 15). *Research.* Retrieved from www
   .schoolofone.org/research.html

7. Rocketship Education. (2010, November). *Our mission: Eliminate
   the achievement gap.* Retrieved from http://rsed.org/index.php?page=
   mission

8. Vander Ark, T. (2010, June 22). *Rocketing to quality at scale.*
   OpenEd Solutions. Retrieved from http://openedsolutions.com/
   rocketing-to-quality-at-scale.html

9. Rocketship Education. (2009, September 16). *Rocketship Education
   2009 academic results highest performing in San Jose and Santa Clara
   County, tops Palo Alto Unified.* Retrieved from http://rsed.org/down
   loads/rsed_09_results_release_9.16.pdf

10. Vander Ark, T. (2011, May 7). *Q&A with John Super, AdvancePath.*
    OpenEd Solutions. Retrieved from http://openedsolutions.com/
    qa-with-john-super-advancepath.html

11. Vander Ark, T. (2010, October 29). *Online partnerships for elementary
    success.* OpenEd Solutions. Retrieved from http://openedsolutions.
    com/online-partnerships-for-elementary-success.html

12. K12. (2010, November 20). *K12 socialization study.* Retrieved from
    http://go.k12.com/b2b/gen/social/?B2b_spnshp=k12_social&B2b_
    plcmt=web&B2b_art=gen&B2b_cta=rpt&B2b_date=20090622

13. Ambient Insight. (2011, January). *2011 learning and performance
    technology research taxonomy: Research methodology, buyer segmenta-
    tion, product definitions, and licensing model.* Retrieved from www
    .ambientinsight.com/Resources/Documents/AmbientInsight_
    Learning_Technology_Taxonomy.pdf

CHAPTER SEVEN: INNOVATION

1. Manno, B. V. (2010, November 29). More families turning to school
   choice. *Education Week.* Retrieved from http://openedsolutions.com/
   edit-blog.html%5D

2. Jacobs, J. (1992). *Systems of survival.* New York: Random House.
   Originally published in 1961.

3. U.S. Department of Education, 2010, November 17, op cit.

CHAPTER EIGHT: INVESTMENT

1. Vander Ark, T. (2009, February 2). *Private capital and public education: Toward quality at scale.* AEI Future of American Education

Project. Working Paper 2009-02. American Enterprise Institute. Retrieved from www.aei.org/docLib/Vander%20Ark.pdf

2. Gold, R. (2009, September 2). *U.S. doles out grants for energy projects.* First Wind. Retrieved from www.firstwind.com/news/us-doles-out-grants-energy-projects

3. Marshall, M. (2009, October 23). *Massive funding to lift smart grid companies. Look for it next month.* VentureBeat. Retrieved from http://venturebeat.com/2009/10/23/massive-funding-to-lift-smart-grid-companies-look-for-it-next-month/

4. Vander Ark, 2009, February 2, op cit.

5. Bush, J., & Wise, B. (2010, December 1). *Digital learning now!* The Foundation for Excellence in Education. Retrieved from http://excelined.org/Docs/Digital%20Learning%20Now%20Report%20FINAL.pdf

6. Cohen. J. (2010). *Who we are.* City Light Capital. Retrieved from www.citylightcap.com/who-we-are/

7. W. K. Kellogg Foundation. (2010). *How we work.* Retrieved from www.wkkf.org/who-we-are/how-we-work/overview.aspx

8. Investors' Circle. (2010, December 16). *Investments in education: An interview with Kim Smith.* Retrieved from www.investorscircle.net/index.php?contentID=3282&categoryID=32&journalID=76

9. Telecom Regulatory Authority of India. (2011, April 29). *Highlights of Telecom subscription data as on 31st March 2011.* Retrieved from www.trai.gov.in/WriteReadData/trai/upload/PressReleases/823/Press_Release_Mar-11.pdf

CHAPTER NINE: EMPLOYMENT

1. Parent Revolution. (2010). *Our mission.* Retrieved from http://parentrevolution.org/?page_id=4

2. Carmichael, G. (2010). *User profile.* Retrieved from http://gailcarmichael.com/

3. Vander Ark, T. (2010, March 6). *Carl Dorvil: A great American story.* OpenEd Solutions. Retrieved from http://openedsolutions.com/carl-dorvil-a-great-american-story.html

4. Laufenberg, 2010, November, op cit.

5. Vander Ark, 2010, October 29, op cit.

6. Setser, B. (2011, January 12). *A perfect storm of reform.* OpenEd Solutions. Retrieved from http://openedsolutions.com/perfect-storm-of-reform.html

7. Wilson, F. (2010, August 22). *The expanding birthrate of web startups.* A VC: Musing of a VC in NYC. Retrieved from www.avc.com/a_vc/2010/08/the-expanding-birthrate-of-web-startups.html

8. Vander Ark, T. (2010, August 26). *Q&A with Nic Borg, Edmodo.* OpenEd Solutions. Retrieved from http://openedsolutions.com/qa-with-nic-borg-edmodo.html

9. Peck, M. S. (1978). *The road less traveled* (p. 15). New York: Touchstone.

CONCLUSION

1. Hess & Manno, 2011, p. 202, op cit.
2. KnowledgeWorks Foundation, 2010, op cit.

APPENDIX

1. Bedell, J. T. *Professional development 2.0: Take control of your own learning.* Amazon Digital Service. Retrieved from www.amazon.com/Professional-Development-2–0-Learning-ebook/dp/B0046ZS304/ref=sr_1_2?ie=UTF8&m=AG56TWVU5XWC2&s=digital-text&qid=1287166686&sr=8–2

2. Bush & Wise, 2010, December 1, op cit.
3. Bush & Wise, 2010, December 1, ibid.

INDEX

create, 101–118; integrating customization, motivation, equalization for, 79–100; just-in-time learning as part of, 6–8; learning revolution driving, 10–13; stimulus grant programs supporting, 8–9; transformational productivity goal of, 116–118. *See also* K–12 school districts; K–12 schools; Learning revolution

Education reform innovation: challenges facing successful, 101–103; overcoming opposition to, 112–114; paying for, 119–141; policies to boost achievement, 103–118; signs of leadership for transformational, 116–118

Education reform policies: accountability, 112; all students are digital learners, 105; college- and career-ready standards and preparation, 103–105; competency-based system, 109–110; educational choice, 105–106; fund kids and not districts, 106–109; new certification standards, 110–112

Educational choice: providing parents with, 105–106; trend toward, 27

Educational crisis: seizing the opportunity to change the, 2; status of the U.S., 2

Educational digital tools: educational equalization through, 64–77; example of digital native

using, 19–21; *Living and Learning with New Media* study findings on, 21–22; the technology available for, 15–17; Ushodaya High (India) use of, 16–17; Web 2.0 applications used as, 35–36. *See also* Technology

Educators: certification of, 110–112; changing notion of traditional, 143–144; new edupreneur role of, 153–156, 160; new job of administration, 152–153; online, 151; parents as, 144–147. *See also* Students; Teaching

Educomp Solutions, 133

Edupreneurs: educator evolution into, 153–155; examples of making a difference, 155–156; shaping the learning landscape, 160

Edusoft, 155

Electronic democracy trend, 27

Empathy Learning Systems, 134

Enterprise Elementary (Washington), 33–34

Enterprising Schools, 133

Envision Schools (San Francisco), 14

Equalization: brief history of access and, 65–67; explosion of learning resources providing, 76–77; of "Growth America" and "Decline America," 63–64; increasing digital content for, 69–71;

we know about learning, 50–52; simulations and impact on, 53–56, 58–60

Moving Learning Games Forward report (Education Arcade), 55

Murdoch, Rupert, 43

Music keystroke data, 38

MyHomeLearning.com, 85

N

N-E-I-E-I-O mnemonic, 99–100

National Association of Software and Service Companies (India), 141

National Educational Technology Plan, 81

National Heritage Academies, 121

National Public Radio, 58

Netflix, 39

New American Schools Development Corporation, 13

New Profit, 129

New Tech Network, 10

New York City Department of Education's Research and Policy Support Group, 86

New York City iZone, 140

New York Times Magazine, 56

News Corporations, 131

NewSchools Venture Fund, 116, 129, 139

No Child Left Behind, 102, 111

Nonprofit organizations: description of, 122; limitations for

school funding by, 121–124; role for education capital investment by, 126

North Carolina Virtual Public School, 153

Nundy, Neera, 17

O

Obama, Barack, 129

Obama stimulus programs, 8–9

OER Commons, 69

O'Hara, Jeff, 154

Online content: capital investment in, 130; CK-12 (free online textbooks), 36; efforts to organize open, 69; Flex model of, 95; instant feedback driven by embedded, 36–38; open education resources (OER), 69, 70; potential for equalization through, 67–71; saving school budget by using open, 69–71; shift toward using, 11

Online courses: blended (or hybrid) schools offering, 80–81; capital investment in, 130–131; first generation of, 35; increasing application of, 80–82; individual progress learning component of, 35; overcoming opposition to, 112–114; providing equal access to students, 67–68; PsPU platform for, 76–77; STEM and AP, 70, 131; teaching, 141; Web 2.0 learning tools used for, 35–36